W9-DBV-067

0 03 03 0082385 0

WITHDRAWN
MENASHA'S PUBLIC LIBRARY

# THE MEANING OF FATIMA

# THE MEANING
## OF
# FATIMA

11560

By
C. C. MARTINDALE, S.J.

NEW YORK
P. J. KENEDY & SONS

COPYRIGHT 1950
BY P. J. KENEDY & SONS
PRINTED IN THE UNITED STATES

232
M36

# CONTENTS

# OFFERED TO OUR BLESSED LADY

SINCE I can never divest myself of the duty of expressing my thanks as best I can to our Blessed Lady, I would wish to offer the following pages to her. When she imparted her message to the children at Fatima, she did so in different measures: she spoke only to Lucia; Jacinta heard her words, but less distinctly; Francisco heard nothing at all. And none of the children could bear to contemplate her steadily, so dazzling was the light that arrayed her. So I, who could but read what others have said about her, must often hesitate and may fall into many a misunderstanding.

I pray then to be preserved from as many of these as possible and to mislead no one. If I do not disguise such obscurities as I shall seem to encounter, no one, I trust, is likely to think that I am saying anything derogatory to our Lady; I shall be recalling how the Bishop of Leiria, when, on May 3, 1922, he initiated the canonical process that was to enquire into the facts of Fatima, quoted Leo XIII's own quotation—that the first law of history was that nothing false must be said, and that no one must fear to tell the truth. Trusting, therefore, to our Lady's guidance, and invoking her also under this, the latest of her many titles, I will try to tell yet again the story of her message transmitted through three children at the Cova da Iria in 1917.

LONDON-FATIMA-SINTRA-LISBON-LONDON, 1947-1949.

# INTRODUCTORY

## I

THE evidence concerning what happened at Fatima in 1917 is of two quite different sorts, and belongs to two widely separated periods.

The first consists of contemporary newspaper-reports—these I have not seen, but they are relatively unimportant, and their substance is used by Fr. De Marchi in the book mentioned below. It is to be found too in two books of the highest value by Canon M. N. Formigão (under the pseudonym 'Visconde de Montelo')—*Os Episodios Maravilhos de Fatima* (1921), and *As Grandes Maravilhas de Fatima* (1927). Meanwhile in 1919 Bishop José Alves Correia da Silva took possession of the resuscitated See of Leiria and set up a canonical enquiry into the story related by the children Lucia, Jacinta and Francisco. Though the Canon had been the first official interrogator of these children, as from September, 1917, the Enquiry included also the depositions of the parish priest of Fatima who had had earlier to question them, and the examination of Lucia herself, the only surviving child, and some other documents. The interrogations made by Canon Formigão himself are included, practically in their entirety, in his second volume.

A totally new sort of evidence began to be provided by Lucia herself in statements or letters beginning in 1925-27, but more fully in two documents (1937-38 : 80 typed pages altogether which have been utilised but not published in full): the former is chiefly about her cousin Jacinta: and more fully still when, as the 'silver jubilee' of the Apparitions drew

near, the Bishop told her to put down in such detail
as she could the history of her experiences: this she
did in two more documents (60 pages) in 1941-42.
A third sealed document remains, not to be opened till
1960, possibly because of references to persons who
will then be no more alive, 'prudential' reasons, too,
have been responsible for certain omissions in what
has already been published (see p. 161). An exhaustive
history of 'Fatima' cannot therefore yet be written;
but enough has appeared to enable us to have
an excellent idea of the occurrences and to form a
justifiably trustworthy opinion about them.

On these various documents, selected persons to
whom they have been shown have based their books.
Notable among these is Fr. L. G. da Fonseca, S.J.,
who, though Portuguese, writes in Italian, and used
them for his *Le Meraviglie de Fatima:* I have the ninth
edition, which in view of many typescript insertions
is really the tenth. The book has had an enormous
circulation and is translated into many languages ;
the author has twice submitted his work to the
criticism of Lucia herself. Dr. J. Galamba de Oliveira
used the documents for his *Jacinta*, of which I have
the 1946 edition: Don L. Moresco did so too for his
*La Madonna di Fatima* (ed. 1-3, 1942). Canon C.
Barthas has adapted Fr. da Fonseca in his *Fatima,
Merveille inouie* (ed. 2, 1943). Fr. Rambaud, O.P.,
*La Dame toute belle* (1949), seeks to make an 'objective
and psychological' account of the events. But the book I
have found most satisfactory is Fr. J. De Marchi's *Era
uma Senhora mais brilhante que o Sol* (ed. 3, 1947):
an abridgement by A. C. Branco and P. C. M.
Kelly, C.S.C., has already appeared in America
(New York, 1947). Fr. De Marchi has lived at Fatima
itself since 1943 and has been able to interrogate not
only Lucia in her convent but most of the surviving

eye-witnesses, including the parents of the two younger children. There are, of course, innumerable other books about Fatima: we may mention Archbishop Ryan's *Our Lady of Fatima* (1943) and the late W. T. Walsh's book with the same title (1948), over which no pain was spared; and *Vision of Fatima* (Boston, 1948) by Fr. T. McGlynn, O.P., a sculptor who, commissioned to make a statue of Our Lady of Fatima as accurately as possible, actually modelled it under the eyes of Lucia herself, obedient to her minutest directions. His book stands by itself, and I shall often have occasion to quote it.

Since Lucia's latter statements have come to light, it has been (I think) the universal practice to interweave them with the contemporary records. It is not always easy to disentangle them. Yet I feel that it is necessary to try to do so if the history of Our Lady of Fatima is to be studied as it reached, step by step, the awareness of the Faithful. A study of the known documents was initiated by Fr. E. Dhanis, S.J., in the Flemish review *Streven* (Vol. xi, pp. 129-149 and 193-215), of which he has kindly lent me the French translation. He has been commented on by Dr. Karrer in the *Schweizer Rundschau* (October, 1947); and in his 'Chronique de spiritualité' in *Nova et Vetera* (May-August, 1948), Mgr. C. Journet of Fribourg strikingly juxtaposes Fr. Dhanis with Fr. da Fonseca and Canon Barthas. Dr. E. K. Winter, late deputy-mayor of Vienna, has kindly sent me a reprint of his article 'Die Russlandbotschaft von Fatima' in the former magazine (fascs. 4 and 5, 1948-49), as well as two long letters on the subject. I have here to add that, since revisiting Fatima, I had the good fortune to meet Fr. De Marchi and to talk over many obscure points with him; but also, I found that he was preparing a fourth edition of his

book which I regard as indispensable, and was able
to consult the draft of an English translation by Mrs.
I. M. Kingsbury, who has already published a short
book in English, *The Miracle of the Mountains*.

Now, given the enormous amount of books already
written about Fatima, and the need of quoting direct
evidence textually so far as possible, it is quite
impossible to avoid writing what other people have
written. On the other hand, one ought not to 'poach'
nor even to repeat more than is necessary what can
be found elsewhere. Therefore I may seem to stress
the psychological elements in this story more than
the pictorial, than the devotional or the moralising.
Nothing, of course, should be omitted because it is
not to one's taste or emphasised because one likes it.
Still, we cannot disguise from ourselves that the story
of Fatima has created difficulties for some readers,
partly, maybe, because they cannot enter into the
imagination of the Portuguese people—let alone, of
upland ignorant peasant children (so different is
that world from our sophisticated one!), but also,
for reasons which seem to them serious and substantial. It is these whom, here and there, we have
in mind. They deserve every attention, if only
because the Message of Fatima—if it be authentic,
as I hold that it is—has world-wide implications to a
degree that even Lourdes, on the face of it, had not.
Therefore I would hope that this short book—in-
exhaustive and here and there inconclusive as it needs
must be—may be regarded as a modest appendix to
the authoritative work of Fr. De Marchi.

## II

Even in so short a book as this, it seems right that
our method of approach to any 'private revelation'

should be made quite clear. God has given, through our Lord, the 'universal', or general, revelation of Himself, and this was closed after the death of the Apostles. Nothing can be added to it. The Church has the mandate to preach it, and the guarantee that this preaching will be 'infallible', i.e. that nothing substantial will be added to it, or subtracted from it, or distorted. Therefore, if God should please to reveal Himself—His truth and His law—to any person whom He may choose, this will not in any way conflict with the Revelation given at the outset to the Apostles. Thus the Church, when examining events like the Apparitions of Fatima, always begins by scrutinising their *dogmatic content*. For instance, we do not *found* our worship of the Sacred Heart of our Lord on the 'private revelations' granted to St. Margaret Mary, nor our belief in the Immaculate Conception on the apparitions that were granted to St. Bernadette at Lourdes. Such events can corroborate, or elucidate, what the Church believes, but cannot add anything to it.

Therefore, it is clear that when ecclesiastical authority 'approves' any special cult, which has had for starting-point some human *story*, the approbation goes straight to the dogmatic essence of what has been 'revealed' and is not concerned with human —perhaps very inadequate—ways of describing the event. Thus Cardinal Lambertini, afterwards Benedict XIV, in his classical *On the Beatification and Canonisation of the Servants of God* (see Book III, c. liii, 15; and II, xxxii, 11), says with special reference to the 'revelations' of St. Hildegarde, St. Bridget and St. Catherine of Siena: 'Such an (ecclesiastical) approbation is nothing else than a permission to publish (a narrative), after mature examination, in view of the instruction and utility of the Faithful. (I have said that) the assent of Catholic Faith to revelations thus approved is not only not obligatory, but *not possible;* (such revelations) demand only an assent of human credence conformably with the rules of human prudence which represents them as probable and piously credible.' The Fifth Provincial Council of Malines (1937) quotes this, and continues: 'Therefore the verdict of the Church does not at all offer these matters as having to be believed by all; it simply declares that they are not contrary to faith or morals, and that there is evidence providing grounds for a pious and prudent assent of human belief'. Canon E. Amort, in his *De revelationibus . . . regulae tutae* (Augsburg, 1744), accumulated an immense mass of documents from which he deduced principles that all agree are accurate, though he applies them with no little severity to, for example, the revelations ascribed to St. Gertrude. Therefore, anyone who is fitted to examine evidence *ought* to do so, especially when some allegedly preternatural event is concerned: but also, any loyal and modest-minded Catholic will be far from lightly rejecting any 'devotion' or cultus that the Holy See has approved, especially if some item or other in the narrative of the event merely clashes with his taste or with what he feels *he* is likely to experience—if only because a Scandinavian, for example, is not likely to think, prefer, or say exactly what a Corsican or a Chinaman would, and a man of science whose life was spent in laboratories would probably not receive the same sort of heavenly illumination as a Portuguese or Patagonian peasant would, or express it in the same sort of language.

In consequence we observe that the Holy See does not base its approbations primarily on the actual words used by recipients of 'private revelations' but on the doctrine they imply, and indeed, sits lightly to the former. Thus the sanction given by the Holy See to a pilgrimage to Our Lady of Pellevoisin, founded in 1876 in consequence of an apparition, is often quoted. In 1900, the Sacred Congregation of Rites approved the 'devotion' in general, but did not hesitate to alter certain details (including the title assumed in the apparition by our Lady herself). The Archbishop of Bourges, in whose territory the apparition had occurred, showed himself more guarded than the faithful would have liked. The Holy Office therefore assured him (September 8, 1904) that the previous approbation implied *no* approbation 'direct or indirect, of no matter what apparitions, revelations, graces of healing and other similar events which in one way or another people may wish to connect with the above-mentioned scapular and above-mentioned pious confraternity'. Thus it will be seen that Pius XII, who is known to be personally devout to Our Lady of Fatima, none the less, in his Portuguese broadcast on October 31, 1942, the 'silver jubilee' of the Apparitions, did not do exactly what Lucia had originally hoped and asked should be done. Benedict XIV admits that things 'unrevealed or even untrue' may be inserted by a quite honest recipient of a quite genuine 'revelation' into his account of it. I am not attending here to the progressive modifications of a story by writers who, consciously or not, wish to improve upon it. Thus there was a period when, for example, St. Margaret Mary's statements were put into a more 'literary' French by those who thought that her 'uncultured' words would displease the better-educated readers of their day: happily the Visitation of Paray has edited her writings exactly as they were written. So too we are now able to read St. Francis Xavier's letters in the form in which he really wrote them. And we are more nearly able now to know what Ste. Thérèse de Lisieux really looked like: many examples of a progressive modification of the original in the interests of current literary taste, or pious preferences, could be adduced, and even of sheer invention. It is *because* I believe firmly in the supernatural origin of the apparitions at Fatima and of the message given by God, through our Lady, that I shall try to reach the essential facts about what happened there. I suggest, therefore, the following points, to which I shall afterwards have to refer back:

1. The more purely spiritual a divine communication—the more directly it is given to the soul, to what has been called the 'fine point' of the soul, or again, the 'centre of the soul'—the more necessary (and difficult) will it be for the recipient to express it even to himself in terms of clear ideas, and it may be almost or quite impossible for him to convey it to others in words. Thus a saint like the Curé d'Ars, overwhelmed by the intensity of his spiritual experience, may yet be able to say only what everyone, in a sense, already knows, such as: 'God is good and loves us: Sin is terrible: Our Lady is all-pure'. Constantly saints have to correct themselves and insist that what they say does not really approximate to what they 'saw', or, like Bd. Angela of Foligno, to cry out 'It wasn't at all like that', when her words had, after all, been taken down one by one by some 'secretary'. Even on the natural plane, we have no words in which to describe the curves of a cyclamen, the scent of a hyacinth, the incomparable colours of some butterfly; still less, why some phrase of music or line of poetry *means* so much to us.

2. Hence a seer may deliberately or unconsciously clothe his 'form-less' vision in imagery or symbolism proper to his time and place but unintelligible, or

even distasteful to men of a different age. Thus most of St. John's Apocalypse would have been clear and congenial to men well acquainted with the Old Testament and with the art and circumstances of nearer-Asiatics, but *we* can hardly decipher parts of it and cannot enjoy various details of it: again, it is only recently that we can use symbols or metaphors drawn from electricity or neurology.

3. Often the recipient may think that his mystical experience is still going on when in reality it has ceased, but he is still 'under the shock of it'. Thus St. Gertrude asked St. Mechtild to obtain the grace of 'patience' for her. Our Lord 'told' St. Mechtild that Gertrude already possessed that virtue, 'patientia' being derived from 'pax' and 'scientia', which it is not. Gertrude must *know* the divine origin of her pains and must keep her soul in *peace* accordingly: thus she would preserve 'patience'. Here certainly you have Mechtild reflecting on the heavenly assurance (as we may surmise) that Gertrude *was* patient.

4. The recipient may either receive his experience in symbolical form or add a symbolical form to that experience and then misinterpret it, as St. Peter did (Acts x. 10) when he saw 'animals clean and unclean' and was told to 'kill and eat', and replied that he had never yet eaten anything 'unclean'; and then was told that what was *meant* was that the Gentiles were not to be excluded from Christ's followers.

5. Such misinterpretation is the easier when what is given spiritually and generally is applied in a concrete and specific way, as when Ste. Jeanne d'Arc thought that the heavenly promise of help and victory meant that she would be delivered from the prison she was in; or when St. Vincent Ferrer declared that he knew for certain that the end of the world was imminent, and (though without sufficient

certainty for him to preach it) that the Antichrist was already nine years old.

6. It is, too, almost impossible for the recipient of some purely spiritual experience not to 'rationalise' it —that is, at least sometimes, to express it in material terms, as when St. John (Apoc. iv. 1), summoned to enter into ecstasy, said that a 'door (into heaven) was opened' and that he was called to 'come up hither'; or even, when the order given concerns something material, it is easy to interpret it in terms of what is already known, as when St. Bernadette was told to go and drink, she assumed that this *must* mean 'from the Gave' which was flowing just behind her, and needed to be corrected and made to scrape away the soil till a few drops of water oozed up.

7. Finally, we all experience that as time goes on we 'arrange' our memories; we discard the unessential, the discordant, the unpleasant; we emphasise instinctively what suits us and put it into a pattern; and even if we deny the validity of some suggestion, it yet may set us off on a new line of thought—thus: 'Did your heavenly voice use such or such a word?' The answer might be a definite 'No', and *then* we might realise that we had not heard words *at all*, but received an interior message only, as when St. Bernadette said that she heard our Lady 'here', i.e. in her heart. All human minds are subject to the same psychological laws, yet each mind will presumably have its own tendencies, so that we cannot tell *a priori* whether a mind is more likely to crystallise its memories and be unable to depart from its earliest impressions, or, to modify them as time goes on and as experience enriches it.

I have been trying to suggest ways in which (as I said) an *honest* witness may misunderstand or misdescribe a *genuine* supernatural experience, and have therefore excluded all reference to illusions, diabolic or, for example, hysterical in origin; and all elements in a 'vision' which are purely due to the imagination of the seer or to the introduction of ideas proper to his time; such imaginative elements would be 'historical', for example, the number of nails used in the Crucifixion or the position of the wound in our Lord's side: such ideas might be that the earth is flat or the heavens a crystal vault. Finally, we have not alluded to the frequently observable cases in which some 'secretary' or editor has altered the words of a 'seer' who has dictated, or even written, his experiences—this may have been done because the seer spoke very fast, or in broken sentences, or because the scribes thought the holy person had been un-orthodox without intending to be so, or simply because they wished to render the document more 'literary' or devotional. Scrupulously exact quotation has been but relatively recently insisted on, and even now is by no means always the rule.[1]

\*    \*    \*

Christian nations have loved to interweave the history of their origin with legends that should never be despised, because they witness to a certain out-look, a vision of the world and of reality. I cannot imagine with what legends the modern nations in process of forming themselves will adorn their recol-lections, save that they will certainly eliminate those sordid elements of which, alas, we are only too well aware. A real substantial fact that went to the

---

[1] Very many more instances of this sort are to be found in Poulain, *Grâces d'Oraison* (xxi, pp. 334-56). I have purposely refrained from quoting 'mystics' of doubtful value, like Maria d'Agreda, Catherine Emmerich, etc.

creation of 'Portugal', and also was productive of
legends, was devotion to our Lady. That Alfonso
Henriques, who detached his lands from the kingdom
of León and became the first king of Portugal, was
born a cripple and miraculously cured by our Lady,
may be a 'legend': it remains that after many defeats
at the hands of the Moors he took Santarém (and
then Lisbon) in 1147, got into touch with St. Bernard
(who was 'carrying that century on his shoulders'),
and founded the monastery of Alcobaça, which, like
all Cistercian monasteries, was dedicated to our
Lady, and in 1152 arranged that an annual tribute
should be sent to Clairvaux. This is not the place to
relate the civilising work done by this monastery
with its army of maybe 800 monks: but, somewhat as
in Hungary, the ultimate source of authority was not
so much the King as the Crown, a crown worn at the
origin by our Lady.

The years went forward, and in 1385 John,
illegitimate son of Pedro I and Grand Master of
Aviz, was, after his victory over the Castilians at
Aljubarrota, acclaimed king by the people. He thereupon vowed to build a church in honour of Our Lady
of the Battle—'Battle Abbey'—and after his marriage
with Philippa of Lancaster, elder daughter of John
of Gaunt, the building actually began, with many
'English' elements, though one cannot be sure of
what plans or architects Philippa herself introduced
from our country. Anyhow, the marvellous construc-
tion was entrusted to the Dominicans, and the
Rosary began to be an integral part of the religious
life of Portugal.

Intermingled with John's life—in fact, what
would it have been without him?—was the 'Holy
Constable', Nuno Alvares Pereira, recently beatified,
who, not far from Ourém, prayed before the battle

of Aljubarrota, when the armies met one another
still fasting, since it was the Vigil of the Assumption.
His only daughter married one of the king's sons
and thus became ancestor of the eighth Duke of
Braganza, founder of that dynasty. Nuno rebuilt in
his home town, Vila Viçosa, a church said to be the
first dedicated in honour of Our Lady's Immaculate
Conception, and built many others of which eight
are well known. Finally he retired to the Lisbon
Carmel which he had built in 1389 and offered his
sword there: the great earthquake has left us nothing
but its ruins: when he is himself better known, maybe
the ruins will be restored—and Portuguese 'restora-
tions' are, so far, often very good.

Pope Boniface IX, at the request of John I,
declared that all the cathedrals of Portugal should
be dedicated in honour of our Lady, and by a pleasing
coincidence this enactment was read out in Lisbon
on a May 13, date of the first Fatima apparition.
The Archbishop of Braga bequeathed great riches to
the church of Our Lady in Guimarães (built by the
father of Henriques) because of the help she had
always given him, especially in the 'Royal Battle',
'where many of us saw her with our own eyes', and
he mentions the often-fulfilled vow of John I to go
barefoot to that church. The Immaculate Conception
became the great devotion of the Braganzas, and
John IV in 1646 renewed the act of his distant ancestor, recognised Our Lady Immaculate as patroness
and defender of the realm, called upon the Cortes
to profess themselves her vassals, himself vowed (and
insisted that the University of Coimbra should do so
too) to defend the belief that Mary was conceived
immaculate, and ordered the continuance of the
annual tribute, 50 gold crowns, to the sanctuary in
Vila Viçosa. Probably all Catholic countries have

liked to maintain that they were in some sense our Lady's best - beloved — certainly England fervently made that claim, and England has the right to say that it supported belief in the Immaculate Conception of Our Lady maybe earlier than any. But it is remarkable how the names just mentioned make a sort of constellation around Fatima. Santarém is to its south; Coimbra rather further to its north: Alcobaça, Batalha, Aljubarrota and the ancient city and see of Leiria to its west, and Ourém and the knightly city of Thomar to its east.

## PART I

CHAPTER I

# THE CHILDREN AND THEIR HOME

SINCE my second visit to Portugal was meant almost entirely for the sake of studying Fatima, I must deny myself any account of the enchanting scenery through which I went to the shrine. But I experienced a shock on finding that you can no more drive right past the colonnade and archways that admitted you to the Cova da Iria.[1] You must swing off to the right by a colossal road that they are building and come back into the village from its further side. That is because the poor Cova is being flattened out and the colonnade and archways exist no more. When first I saw the Cova it was still a huge saucer-like depression and the massive stone causeways built across it rather like spokes of a wheel projecting from the central fountain left fairly deep hollows between them where olives and holm-oaks grew and people might bivouac in at least a filigree of shade. Today there is only a vast expanse of earth and stones—the very idea of walking across this might terrify you. Doubtless avenues will be planted here, just as trees are being put alongside the new road; but where they will find water, who can tell? The Basilica, dazzling white, is even now not quite finished: but to the left is the very fine red-roofed

[1] The scene of the apparitions. 'Cova' means 'hollow', and Iria is the name of an ancient martyr which has made its way into many other place-names round about.

hospital with the retreat-house and hostel behind it; and to the right another similar hospital is all but completed. The source in the middle still exists under its circular building topped by a column with the gilt statue of the Sacred Heart above it; but it has been stripped of its wide verandah and I could not see how people now drew the water—anyhow in this year of drought there was hardly any anywhere. The only unchanged item is the tiny chapel of the Apparitions—really, just a shed: you enter by a small vestibule built over the stump of the *carras-queira* tree where our Lady stood—the stump, if it still exists, has a sort of stone chest covering it; an opening was left through which it was hoped new shoots would find an exit; but no: it must be quite dead. The other part consists of a minute chapel with room for little more than the celebrant and two or three worshippers. Much better to say your prayers in the dust outside.

It is always a pleasure to *recognise* friendly places and people, and to receive so friendly a welcome as Mrs. Petrarcchi's in her *pousada:* I had the same room as last time, but, to myself, evacuating it only for the pilgrimage of August 13, when it was occupied by *four* young men. During that time I emigrated to the Seminary of which a third is built, and by a first gift of Providence met there and elsewhere Fr. De Marchi, who was in Fatima for just those three days on his way from the United States to Italy. The priests here are Italian *Consolata* Fathers and most genial and informative. The rooms are large and airy and spotlessly clean, and when the building is finished it will be on a vast scale, simple, practical and dignified. As for me, I left to one side the great ceremonies, save for the Procession, for the heat came down like a hammer, and on the last day was thunderous till a terrific rain-burst cleared the air. Therefore I made most of my visits to the Cova quite early or quite late.

Our first expedition was naturally to Aljustrel, about a kilometre and a half distant, the tiny hamlet where the three favoured children were born. The country is said to be very like Palestine, at least so far as stoniness goes. Small fields are divided by low stone walls—much less compact than those of our own North Country—and the shallow soil needs a lot of de-stoning before it can be cultivated. In the spring there must be much fruit-tree blossom and the loveliest wild-flowers, not least the wild peony of which Jacinta grew so fond. But naturally in August there was none of this; the green was that of olive-trees and dim metallic evergreens, and the glare off the rocks and reddish earth was fatiguing. The few houses are one-storied, either dazzlingly white-washed (or at least the frameworks of doors or windows are), or bare stone or stone covered with thin stucco. The interiors are perfectly clean (so far as I could judge), and contain very little but solid and evidently ancestral furniture and a wonderful collection of pots, pans and brooms and usually, especially in one room, any amount of holy pictures. You would say, a preferred simplicity rather than an enforced poverty: in fact, these small land-holders are neither affluent nor 'poor'.

On the right of the narrow twisting road is the house where the parents of Jacinta and Francisco used to live, and almost just opposite it is that in which they actually do. A little further on, upon the left, is the house where Antonio dos Santos (d. July 31, 1919) lived with his wife Maria Rosa (d. July 7, 1942). They had six children, one boy and five girls, of whom Lucia was the youngest: she was born on

March 22, 1907. It appears that as often as not
Portuguese peasants are even better known by nick-
names than by their surnames, and Antonio was
affectionately known as Abóbora, the Pumpkin—not,
I hasten to say, because of his shape, but because he
came from a place where pumpkins grew exceptionally well.

The family owned several patches of land round
about which they cultivated or where they grazed
their sheep on such rough vegetation as could force
its way up between the stones. However, Abóbora,
though genial and well-liked, was 'fonder of the wine-
shop than of the church': to make up, Maria Rosa
was a magnificent character and worked doubly
hard: loving her children deeply, she yet brought
them up very strictly and was quite ready to thrash
them if they were disobedient, and especially if they
told the smallest lie. The only photograph I have
seen of her is taken in her old age, and is certainly
grim, but you see the possibility of the friendliest,
dryly humorous smile.

Lucia's eldest sister, Maria dos Anjos, had for-
tunately returned there the very day I came: but
there were a lot of people present and she was occupied
in selling souvenirs, and I contented myself with
watching her robust and friendly features and
deliberate, accurate hands as she dealt with woven
table-cloths and smaller pieties. She was at the
moment in the house occupied by the Marto family,
Sr. Emanuelo Marto and his wife Olimpia, both
happily still alive.

Olimpia had been married before and had had
two children by her first husband, who died on
October 10, 1895. By her second marriage she had
nine, of whom the youngest was Francisco, born
June 11, 1908, and Jacinta, born March 11, 1910.

Olimpia, though by now very old, is incredibly vivacious and voluble: by a happy chance Sr. Marto (affectionately called 'Ti Marto' by everyone—'ti' really means 'uncle') was away when we arrived, but returned from an expedition to buy shoes well before we left. He too is very gay and kindly, but you see why he was nicknamed 'The Thinker' —*o pensador*—and I thought he was a little bewildered by the crowds who relentlessly asked him and his wife questions they had answered a hundred thousand times. In fact, I thought that these two old people must have led during these thronged days of pilgrimage a quite appalling life and have ended each day exhausted. All the more did I marvel how upright they stood; how completely unflustered they were; how, never having profited one penny by the offers showered upon them, they retained their independence and dignity in poverty and, we must insist, have never deviated one hair's-breadth from the story they originally told, despite the massive suggestion they have received from those who came to learn the amazing destiny of their children. It is these old people, and the characters of those children, which first attracted me, and still do, to the whole story of Fatima.

Fatima itself is about another kilometre and a half further on. The back of the little church remains as it was in Lucia's time; the façade and nave, which were charmingly baroque and irregular, with a bell-turret to one side and two arches on the right, have been demolished and built up in banal Noah's ark style, with a small pointed steeple in the middle. But inside, you are in a proper Portuguese church, full of saints though with the Sacred Heart predominant and not only, I thought, because that feast was to be celebrated in a day or two (August) for the sake of agriculturists who couldn't have come earlier. Hence the church was grandly decorated with hangings rather like bedspreads dependent from the choir-loft and bunches of bright material put here and there upon the pillars. Here was Our Lady of the Rosary that the children saw; a very large picture. of Our Lady of Mount Carmel (re-painted, I felt sure) with angels lifting souls out of purgatorial flames; a little St. Silvester and St. Quiteria (people called her St. Agnes but she had a great dog beside her) and a St. Sebastian.

Though it was late morning, the church was dotted with people at their prayers—not only old men or women, but some quite young men and a boy who knelt in the middle of the pavement really praying and quite inattentive to our invasion. However, one old man did come up to me, to ask (I assumed) for alms. But no. He wanted me to make the Stations of the Cross with him, and when it was explained that I was a stranger, he went away sorrowful.

We then crossed the dusty little square to the cemetery where an inscription candidly observed: 'We bones lie here, awaiting yours.' Immediately to the right, on entering, you see the little stone sarcophagus, already grey and lichened, and you read that 'Here repose the mortal remains of Francisco and Jacinta to whom our Lady appeared'. Attached to the head of this is a sort of canopied edifice open on three sides and surmounted by a cross. It contains a few pious objects—pictures or some flowers—but there is no question of a premature public cultus, though pilgrims undisguisedly chip lumps off the humble stone. As we went back to our car, the Angelus rang, and three husky young men went into the church to pray.

This was our only expedition save to Leiria,

which, lying much lower by the river Lis, was rich in maize-crops. My hostess was fetching a Fatima Madonna that had been carved for the diocese of Brentwood, where, I believe, it is to go on pilgrimage from church to church. Just before I left England I had been to Westminster Cathedral where another such Madonna had established herself, the gift of the Duke and Duchess of Palmella and their family. This too is to move around, I am told, till it finds its definitive place, as at present arranged, in St. James's, Spanish Place.

I asked how it was that this simple, dignified religious life seemed to survive so much better here than in other much more fertile parts of Portugal that I had heard of. I was told that probably it was due to the fact that most of these uplanders were small proprietors and could probably live quite well on their own grain, olives, figs and an occasional meat-meal, whereas elsewhere a more densely populated district might have none but 'seasonal' employment, i.e. during harvest-time or the vintage on land which was not their own, though their pay and 'keep' might be quite good. But the rest of the year they would live in idleness and squalor, uneducated and often priestless, so that vice and communist clichés would get an easier hold on them.

Into such an environment Lucia was born on March 22, 1907. She was a small child all of quick-silver, always wriggling out of her mother's arms and then running back to be cuddled. She kept this up till she was quite big: they chaffed her—'Here she comes to be petted and patted!' But if she liked being treated as a baby, she on her side worshipped babies. When her eldest sister Maria dos Anjos's baby was born, Lucia would race home from wherever she was to cover it with kisses, 'not at all

like the people round here', said Maria somewhat
caustically: I take it that these sturdy folk were not
demonstrative. And children for their part were
devoted to Lucia. Mothers could leave them in
Lucia's charge: if Lucia were there, her sisters Maria
and Carolina could go on with their weaving and
dress-making and even when Lucia was 'quite tiny'
they need not fear to be distracted from their work.
She loved games, but when she was tired of playing
the children would sit under the fig-trees and she
would tell them stories—sometimes well-known ones
(children constantly require to be told what they
know perfectly well already: no word must be altered)
or else, some that she invented. 'She was', said her
uncle Ti Marto, 'a chatterbox and never still for a
minute. She was affectionate, too—even with me.'
(But who could not have been?) 'She was very mis-
chievous', he went on, 'and I often thought she will
be very good or very bad.' She confessed afterwards,
with that sort of blunt humour which became hers,
that she had not only liked putting on all her bright
shawls and trinkets for 'festas' but was pleased that
nobody in that neighbourhood was so gaily dressed
as she and that her sisters and her god-mother Teresa
'were surprised to see me looking so nice'. (We
cannot but smile at this, for indeed her features were
not attractive. Her eyebrows were very thick and
almost met: her nose, they say, was rather flat, and
her lips, too thick.)

Maria Rosa educated her children with affectionate severity. She could, says Maria dos Anjos,
read print but not write. Every evening she would
read part of the Old Testament or the Gospels or
some story such as the apparitions of our Lady at
Nazaré (a Portuguese fishing-village) or Lourdes; and
in Lent the readings would be about the Passion.

Maria Rosa was determined that the children should not only know the catechism by heart but understand the meaning of each word. She did not want to feel ashamed when the priest questioned them. Nor had she need to be—they asked her endless questions, and found that she answered them 'better' even than the priest in church. In fact, this priest had the wise custom of making older children explain the catechism to the younger ones: Maria dos Anjos was a little catechist when only nine. Other children and even grown-ups from other villages too used to come to that house for 'instruction'. As an instance of the questions that might be asked and of the answers given, we might quote Maria dos Anjos: she wanted to know why the fire of hell did not destroy the souls there like wood. Maria Rosa answered that a bone, thrown into the fire, seemed to burn and yet was not consumed.

In May, November and Lent they always said the rosary together and were told to take their beads when they went out with the flocks and to say them after their lunch and to add some *Paters* in honour of St. Anthony lest the sheep should be lost. They also said: 'All holy thanks and praise—be given to Jesus Christ our Lord—for all the benefits and blessings He has given us—Be they given to His honour and praise—for the love of God our Lord.' And they added some *Paters* for the souls of those with whom they had been in any way connected. When they woke, they made acts of contrition and said the Our Father several times and invoked their Guardian Angel who kept them safe night and day and never left their side. Maria Rosa's children were to grow up hard-working and content with their state of life, and above all, never to tell a lie. 'The tiniest fib meant the broom-stick for us!' This ingrained habit of telling the truth is worth remembering in view of the strange story they would have to relate one day.

Francisco, who was born on June 11, 1908, was a sturdy little boy with a round face, a small mouth, and, they say, a well-formed chin. It may be a pity that we have only two photographs, I think, of the three children, both of them very 'arranged'. In one, dated September, 1917, they are standing under the little wooden arch erected above the place of the apparitions among various people, all but two of whom are manifestly not peasants. The two little girls are rather dressed up and look to me very ill-tempered: Francisco is standing, feet firmly apart but rather turned in, his hands clasped, and with cropped hair growing in a peak down on to his forehead. He is frowning a little and his mouth is a straight line, but though he is disliking the experience he is not sulky. But in the better-known photograph of the children—Francisco in the middle, Lucia on the right—I think they have the sun in their eyes and are definitely resentful of the whole performance. No one who remembers the misery of being photographed when a child can be surprised at this! The girls wear heavy veils, voluminous skirts and bodices, and their eyebrows are perfectly straight: Francisco has a short coat, clumsy chequered trousers and his 'stocking-cap' hanging down on to his right shoulder: he holds a long staff. The corners of the mouth of each are definitely turned down in, to me, a most realistic and indignant way.

Lucia and his father suggest different sides of Francisco's character. Ti Marto records him as lively—'What a man he would have been!' exclaimed his mother to Fr. De Marchi—he could stand up against others better even than Lucia could: he went out in the dark without fear: he liked to hunt snakes and lizards and moles—even his mother was alarmed when he brought them back into the house. Once when one of his brothers was snoring, the boy was about to put a bit of wood into his mouth: Ti Marto stopped him: 'I like things to be as they should be! A look was enough. If a donkey kicks you, you needn't cut off his leg!' Once he wouldn't say his prayers: Ti Marto went after him . . . he returned with due docility. (Yet after the Apparitions, he and Jacinta would almost force the family to say the rosary together.) Lucia said he was a great contrast to Jacinta, who was always lively and even capricious. When playing he was not keen enough about *winning*: so he was dull to play with. He would sometimes break off from a game. 'Why?' 'Because you're bad. Because I don't want to go on.' She would be almost irritated and order him off to sit on a stone or the ground. Then she would be sorry and fetch him back: he would return without any bearing of malice. His god-mother brought him a handker-chief with Our Lady of Nazaré stamped upon it: he treasured it: it disappeared: another boy had taken it.

'Let him keep it: *I* don't mind.'

When, rather later, early in 1917, he was sent to school, a fellow schoolboy who afterwards became a seminarian remembers him as backward at first, quiet, and liking to play with one or two only. When the apparitions began he was treated roughly by the teacher—'a good professor but a bad educator' —and bullied by the bigger boys who hemmed him up against a wall during the recreation. He was genuinely sensitive, especially about truth. Once his mother told him to take the sheep to his god-mother's terrain. He refused: 'Are you teaching me to steal?' But next day, he heard that he might always go. He played his little pipe well and could imitate birds but would not take them off their nests. He loved flowers and *light*. He marvelled at the Lamps of Our Lady and the Angels—the moon and stars; but he loved Our Lord's Lamp best: he liked light seen 'through glass' (prisms?) and in dewdrops. Yet this is the same little boy who hunted snakes and scared his mother with them.

Lucia, a dominant personality, to some extent quelled him as his father did not: and yet it was Ti Marto who was the 'Thinker'; whose mind, for all his practical habit, turned inwards: and it was with Ti Marto's help that we shall best be able to 'check' most of what can be said about the last days of Francisco's life.

Jacinta seems to me, at first, more elusive and yet very simple. Her mother says that she was not so plump as Francisco and that her eyes were lighter. She liked having her hair tidy and her mother 'did' it for her every day, and was proud of always having been able to keep her children shod. Jacinta was sensitive, and she cried bitterly even at the age of five when she heard the Passion read and would resolve not to make our Lord suffer any more. She came definitely under the spell of Lucia and clung almost literally to her skirts: when Lucia, at ten, was taken away from play and put to look after the sheep, Jacinta was so inconsolable that after a while her mother gave her a few sheep that she might take them along with Lucia's. Lucia says, in fact, that Jacinta, having seen children dressed as 'angels' throwing flowers before the Blessed Sacrament, gathered flowers and strewed them before *her*. 'That is what the angels did.' (Another time, when herself an 'angel', she strewed no flowers before the Monstrance and kept staring at the priest. She had to be

taught that she must not expect to *see* Jesus in the
Sacred Host: He was hidden there. This, I think, was
the beginning of her and Francisco's devotion to the
'Hidden Jesus'.) Ti Marto says that she was the
sweetest of his children. She gave no trouuble but let
us know 'what she wanted in her own way . . . one
little cry and then no more fuss'.

One would almost say that truthfulness was the
royal virtue in these families. If Olimpia said something such as that she was just going to the cabbage-
patch when really she was going much further,
Jacinta always noticed it and 'scolded her'. 'I myself',
said her father, 'never deceived them like that.'

The affectionate child had a special love for her
lambs: she called them each by its name—the
prettiest names she knew—Dove, Star, Snow—and
would sit petting them and carry them back on her
shoulders and in her arms lest they should grow tired,
and to be like the Good Shepherd of whom she had
a picture. She loved flowers too, and would weave
them into wreaths for Lucia; and would challenge
Francisco to count the stars, herself loving 'Our
Lady's Lamp' best because she could watch the
moon without hurting her eyes. She had a sweet
strong voice and would love to arouse the echoes in
the Serra—the name that echoed best was Maria.
Both she and Lucia loved dancing—'any instrument
was enough to set us off'; but Jacinta was far the more
graceful. Not but that this rather angelic child had
more human qualities. She could definitely sulk and
would not return to play till she had chosen the
game and whom she would play with. . . . There
was a mysterious game called 'buttons': apparently
the buttons on their frocks were played for and won:
Jacinta would constantly win Lucia's and not give
them back so as to have them ready for the next

game. Whereupon Lucia got into trouble with Maria Rosa.

He is brave indeed who imagines that he can enter into the mind of any little child. But who can guess what the mind of these small Portuguese peasants can have been like? What horizons had their 'world'? with whom was it populated? The pages that Maria Rosa read to them took them into the enchanted lands of holy apparitions and of the divine happenings of the Gospel, and these exercise their own special power. But it will be very hard for us even to begin to make contact with these little souls, at once so simple and so spiritual.

## CHAPTER 2

## THE FIRST THREE APPARITIONS

IN what follows, I recall that I try to make sure of how the 'history' of the Apparitions reached the attention of contemporaries. This may not be the best method, and will certainly involve many repetitions and 'flash backs' in the second part of this book. It may be an impossible task to disentangle what was said at first and what was said about it later; still, one can hardly go wrong in distinguishing sentences which were undoubtedly spoken by the children from those which exhibit the vocabulary, turns of speech and forms of thought which became proper to Lucia after years of convent-education.

As time passed, Lucia's home did not become more cheerful. Her father took less and less care of his possessions; and, when Portugal entered the war in 1916 his son Manuel was drafted off into the army and the older girls had to earn what they could by indoor work, and this was when Lucia was put to look after the sheep. She had already made her First Communion at the incredibly early age of six; the parish priest had wanted to put it off; but the venerated Fr. Cruz, lately deceased, happened to be in Fatima and assured him that the child knew her 'doctrine' perfectly. This always remained a happy memory with her: she felt that our Lord was pleased with her and that Our Lady of the Rosary had smiled on her. Soon enough, of course, Jacinta wanted to make her First Communion too; but she was judged too young; as for Francisco, he got

muddled in the Creed, and the priest—who clearly
took instruction seriously—sent him home in tears.
Lucia used to try to teach Jacinta what she could
not understand. It was Lucia who explained why
our Lord could not be *seen* in the Sacred Host; and
when Jacinta went on to ask how so many people
could receive the Hidden Child—did each receive
a little?—Lucia had to say that the Child was hidden
in each and every particle. This theology, for the
while, sufficed: and indeed it may do so for ourselves.
Would that we, who look at the selfsame stars as the
children did, could see them *as* they did, and not
through the blurred spectacles of use and wont, or
even those of scientific astronomy! All the same, joy
seemed to have left the house. Even a new parish
priest arrived who prohibited dancing—save, perhaps,
at home. The people were puzzled: if dancing had
not been a sin before, how could it be so now? Maria
Rosa did not profess to know, but her veneration for
the priesthood was always profound, and, indeed,
this was to be a reason for her to resist Lucia's tales
of 'apparitions' later on, seeing that the priest did not
believe in them.[1]

May 13, 1917, was the Sunday before Ascension
Day. Of course everyone first went to Mass, rain or
fine, even if Mass had to be said in some quite distant
village. Never, says Olimpia, would we miss Mass
even when I had children at the breast. Not that the
really small ones who could just walk were taken:
'You think you're taking a little angel with you and
it turns out a regular little devil.' On this day, after
their breakfast of vegetable soup and bread with a
little olive oil, the three children went off, carrying

[1] I cannot think that the dances in these upland districts can have
been so very scandalous, else Maria Rosa, who was shrewd as well as
strict, would have perfectly well known why they were prohibited.

their lunch, which was much the same—bread, olives and perhaps a sardine. After their lunch of which they kept the scraps for later on, they said the rosary; but to get it over quick these still sub-angelic children said just the two words 'Our Father' and 'Hail Mary' on the larger and smaller beads, and no more. Luncheon and prayer over, they began to build a little house in the Cova da Iria to which they had gone.

While they were playing, there was a flash of lightning (as Lucia said later, 'what we called lightning for want of a better word'). They looked up, but the sky was perfectly clear. All the same, Lucia said, they had better go home: a storm might be brewing. They started, but another brighter flash followed, and they looked without knowing why, towards the right. And they saw a young girl, dressed in white, standing on a *carrasqueira* tree.[1]

The Vision said: 'Don't be frightened: I won't hurt you.'

Lucia said: 'Where do you come from?'[2]

'I come from heaven', and she pointed to the sky.

'And what do you want of me?'

'I have come to ask you to come here the next six months, on the 13th, at this same hour. Afterwards I will tell you who I am and what I want. And I will come back here a seventh time.'

Lucia said: 'And shall I go to heaven too?'

'Yes.'

'And Jacinta?'

[1] An *azinheira* is a sort of holm-oak, prolific in acorns. When younger it can be called a *carrasqueira*, which, it seems to me, is the word Francisco mostly used. This tree was about the same height as Lucia herself.

[2] She used the term *Vocemece*, which is, technically, 'Your Ladyship' or some such expression, but can be used, I am told, by anyone to anyone. Still, it is a politer form than the simple 'you'.

'Yes.'

'And Francisco?'

'Yes; but he will have to say many rosaries.'

Francisco, so far, had not seen the vision, and though he had seen Lucia speaking, neither then nor afterwards did he hear the Vision speak. Lucia remembered two girls who used to come to the house to learn to cook or weave and who had recently died. She said:

'And Maria das Neves—is she in heaven?'

'Yes.'

'And Amelia?'

'She is still in Purgatory.'[1]

Francisco at first did not see the Vision and said: 'Throw a stone at it!' Jacinta in her simplicity wondered if they should not offer it some of their remaining bread and cheese.[2]

The Lady then said (though I do not think that this emerges from the earliest interrogatories): 'Will you offer yourselves to God to submit to all the sufferings that He will send you in reparation for sins by which He is offended and in supplication for the conversion of sinners?'

Lucia said they would.

'Then', said the Vision, 'you will have much to suffer, but the grace of God will be your strength'.

She added that they must say the rosary (*o terco:* five decades) daily to obtain peace for the world and the end of the war. She then moved quietly off

---

[1] The documents present this in three forms. 'She is in Purgatory: She is still in Purgatory: She is in Purgatory till the end of the world.' Lucia has been interrogated about this and has insisted that the third form is correct and that it is not remarkable since you can go to hell for missing Mass on a Sunday.

[2] Lucia is said not to like the mention of this, but does not deny that it happened. Cf. the offer of eau de Cologne (p. 62), and of pen and ink at Lourdes.

towards the east and the dazzling light by which she was surrounded disappeared.

When they recovered themselves they noticed with relief that the sheep were peacefully browsing and they had no more fear of storms. Lucia said she was sure that Jacinta would tell everyone about this; Jacinta vowed she wouldn't. On the way home, Lucia again insisted upon silence. 'I won't tell even Mother', said the child. At the gate of Ti Marto's home Lucia repeated: 'Not even your mother.'[1]

Lucia kept to her resolution and went to bed. But Jacinta, whose parents had gone to Batalha to buy a pig, waited at the gate for their return, and when she saw them, she rushed out, clasped her mother round the knees as she had never done before, says Olimpia, and exclaimed:

'Oh Mother! I saw our Lady today at Cova da Iria!'

'That's likely! A fine saint you are, to see our Lady!'

' But I *saw* her!'

She went on to tell of the lightning and how it frightened them, of the light, of the Lady—such a beautiful Lady—of Francisco who couldn't see at first; of the Lady in such a light that you couldn't look at it, it would blind you; of the rosary to be said daily.

Olimpia was hardly attending and went to prepare some food for the pig, and her husband had gone to

[1] So far, I have used only the word 'Vision', because the children had not yet described it to anyone and because 'Lady' seemed rather too grown-up for someone who, the children afterwards said, looked about fifteen or eighteen. (Bernadette, too, saw our Lady as quite a young girl.) Sometimes they used the untranslatable word *mulherzinha*, i.e. the word for 'woman' ending with the affectionate diminutive of which the Portuguese are so fond. But now I will simply say 'the Lady' save when one of the children or someone else explicitly says 'Our Lady.'

see how 'it was getting on with the other animals'.
Then they came back for supper, which Ti Marto ate
by the fire. His brother-in-law was there and, Olimpia
thinks, all her children.

'Tell us your story again', she said to the child.

Jacinta said, very simply, that there had been a
most beautiful lady, in white, with a gold cord
hanging from neck to waist, her head covered with a
veil or mantle, white—white—whiter than milk; it
fell to her feet and was edged with gold. Her hands
were joined 'like this'—Jacinta stood up and put her
hands together before her breast. She had a rosary
that shone like the stars with a shining cross. She
spoke to Lucia but not to herself nor Francisco—we
must say the rosary every day, and she would take us
to heaven, 'and other things that I can't remember
but Lucia knows. When she went back to heaven the
doors shut so fast that I thought her feet would be
caught. It is so lovely in heaven! There are so many
wild peonies there. . . .'

Francisco agreed with all this: the boys were
inclined to tease; the girls were 'interested'. Ti
Marto's brother-in-law thought that if a lady in
white had appeared it must be our Lady: Olimpia
still laughed. Ti Marto says he reflected that 'since
the beginning of the world our Lady has been appearing at different times and in different ways. Otherwise the world would have been even worse than it
is. These have been the important things. The
power of God is great. We don't understand everything, but God's will be done.' The one thing he was
sure of was that his children were not lying.

In a village like Aljustrel everything is known in
no time. Early next day someone went to see Maria
Rosa who went straight to Lucia, sitting under a
fig-tree 'doing I forget what'.

'I've heard that you saw our Lady in the Cova da Iria. Is that true?'

'Who told you? And I told Jacinta so often not to tell anyone!'

'Why?'

'Because I don't know whether it was our Lady, though it was a lovely little lady (*mulherzinha*). . . . She said we were to come six months running and later she would tell us what she wanted . . . she said she came from heaven.'

Maria Rosa almost forced her to say more but she didn't want to—'I don't think I ever saw her so sad.'

Francisco corroborated the story but Maria Rosa began to fear, and afterwards to feel certain, that her daughter was a liar.

No wonder the children felt depressed and that later in the day when Lucia told Jacinta who was sitting melancholy to come and play, the child said she didn't want to.

'Why not?'

'Because the lady told us to say the rosary and make sacrifices for sinners. And when we say the rosary, we ought to say the whole of it. And sacrifices —how shall we make them?'

Lucia wrote, long afterwards, that they began by giving their lunch to the sheep and later on to poorer children. Francisco, to make up, climbed a tree to pick acorns but Jacinta remembered that another sort of oak had acorns still more bitter. Their lunch, therefore, began to consist of acorns, the heart of pine-cones, roots, blackberries and a little fruit if they were near home. I find it hard not to suppose that Lucia has here somewhat telescoped her memories, because so far as the documents go the word 'sacrifice' had not yet been mentioned. I am far from doubting that the children increasingly practised 'penances', at least when by themselves, for Ti Marto says emphatically that no difference was observed in them after and before the Apparitions.

In February, 1946, a Dutch Montfortian, Fr. Jongen, catechised Lucia (then in her convent) about this.

'What difference do you expect?' she asked with her usual bluntness. 'We continued to play as before. A few pious persons said that if we had seen the Blessed Virgin we ought not to play any more. But what could we do but play? Ought we to have stayed motionless, like our Foundress over her altar?'

But 'voluntary penances' would have been as nothing compared with what Lucia had to suffer from her own family. Ti Marto was much gentler with his two children. He was, so to say, too sceptic to commit himself to the sceptics. Abóbora was indifferent. Maria Rosa was convinced that Lucia was telling lies, and this appalled her. She tried everything—the 'broomstick' included—to force her into saying she had lied. As for Francisco, he told Jacinta it was all her fault for having talked. So they were all sufficiently unhappy.

June 13 approached—the feast of St. Anthony of Lisbon (usually called 'of Padua'), patron of all Portugal. This is celebrated by High Masses, sermons, decorated carts, beflagging of streets, rockets, bombs and all the apparatus that the Portuguese love. Criticism had been running high: the children ought to be dosed with castor-oil; boys shouted at them, 'Look! there's our Lady on the roof!' The local priest, or 'Prior', Don Manuel Marques Ferreira, held his tongue. But it seemed certain that the children *must* go to the festa of St. Anthony! However,

THE FIRST THREE APPARITIONS

we have the eyewitness of Senhora Maria dos Santos Carreira, who died so recently as March, 1949, and who became by reason of her life-time devotion to these events known as Maria da Capelinha—'of the Chapel'. She, though at the time very weak, was resolved to witness what might happen at Cova da Iria on the 13th. At home, Lucia's relatives decided to speak of nothing but the feast to which Lucia had loved going: by the day itself, she would have forgotten all about the Cova. However, the children were determined to go to it as bidden. (This in itself is a very substantial argument in the 'Vision's' favour.) Jacinta even tried to persuade her mother to go too.

Maria Rosa said: 'Don't you want to go to St. Anthony?'

'St. Anthony's no good.'

'No good?'

'The Lady is so much better. I'd go to St. Anthony if the Lady told me to.'

Ti Marto liked neither the idea of going with the children nor letting them go alone. For once—with all respect—he shirked. He and his wife would go to Pedreira and buy some oxen. 'When we get home, the whole affair will be finished with one way or the other.'

The children left early, fed the sheep at a place called Valinhos where there was more grass, brought them home to their pens and changed their clothes. Maria Rosa felt sure that Lucia would go to the festa, but decided that if she did not she would follow to the Cova and hide: at least she would be able to protect her. Lucia in fact started for Fatima to meet some other children—fellow-First-Communicants. Maria Rosa encountered some other people going *away* from Fatima: they said they were looking for the house of

the children who had seen our Lady. Maria Rosa
merely said that they lived at Aljustrel and would be
going to the festa. But she was upset. If now she
went to the Cova she would be recognised and could
not hide.

Meanwhile, Lucia met about fourteen of her little
friends, and they all decided to go back with her:
'when Lucia proposed a thing, no one contradicted
her.' Her brother offered her money not to go; but
go they did. Maria Carreira arrived with her crippled
son João. The children appeared at about eleven.
People offered them oranges; each took one but did
not eat it. Maria Carreira began to feel exhausted and
asked if the Lady would come soon. Lucia said yes,
and shortly afterwards saw the 'flash' and told Jacinta.
They ran to the tree. Others followed them and heard
Lucia say:

'You told me to come here; do me the kindness to
say what you want.'

Thereupon, Maria Carreira said, they heard a very
small voice, but no word was distinguishable: 'it
was like the buzzing of a bee.'[1]

The Lady said that she wished them to come on
the 13th of each month and to say the rosary, inter-
polating between each mystery: 'O my Jesus, forgive
us; deliver us from the fire of hell; take all souls to
heaven, especially those in most need.'

A different form of this prayer became current:
'Deliver the souls in Purgatory, especially those that
are most abandoned': I am told that the change was
due, first, to the use of the word *alminhas* (the kindly
diminutive alluded to above, and currently used of

[1] It was not only now that this curious experience occurred. Ti
Marto was to speak of a 'horsefly in a bottle'. During an English
pilgrimage in 1948 Maria dos Anjos poked a stick into a bees' nest and
out swarmed the bees, all buzzing. 'It was just like that', she said,
delighted, and not worrying that a bee had stung one of the pilgrims.

the 'poor souls' in Purgatory) instead of Lucia's word *almas:* in any case, it is certain that she meant the souls in greatest danger of being lost.

The Lady also told her to learn to read, and 'afterwards I will say what I want'. Lucia asked her to cure a sick person: she answered that if she was converted she would be cured within the year.

'Will you take us to heaven?'

'Yes; soon I will take Francisco and Jacinta. But you must wait here still for some time.'

What else Lucia reported her as having said will be written in the second part of this book.

Lucia then stood up, pointed, and said: 'Look! there she goes!'

Maria Carreira said they heard 'a sound like a rocket, a long way off'. They also saw a small cloud drifting eastward from the tree.

Lucia cried: 'There! Now she can no more be seen. Now she is entering heaven. Now the doors are shut.'

The spectators said that the twigs on the top of the *carrasqueira* were bent eastward as though someone had moved away off it. Maria dos Anjos said it looked like a flat hat. Lucia afterwards said she had not seen this nor yet the cloud. Maria Carreira further said later on that on one occasion she asked Lucia why our Lady never spoke to Jacinta. Lucia said: 'Because Jacinta's tongue is tied. If she spoke, our Lady would speak to her.' Jacinta simply looked at Maria and then at Lucia and smiled shyly. On the way home, these visitors to the Cova met those who were returning from the festa, and thus the news spread wider than ever.

Somehow it was rumoured that the children had been told a 'secret', and this made people more inquisitive than ever. The children did not mind speaking of the Lady's beauty. She was more beautiful than any image in the church. Actually, in August, five ladies arrived at the presbytery, among them a girl of about fifteen dressed in white. They asked the priest to come with them to the Marto's home, where Jacinta was all alone. The poor child was asked whether the Lady was like one of these, like the girl in white. 'No, no! This is a beautiful lady but the one I saw was much more beautiful.'

But as for the 'secret', Ti Marto says that all the women wanted to know it; *he* never asked: 'A secret is a secret and must be kept.' People actually tried to bribe the children with necklaces and other gold ornaments. They never would yield, though, like any children, they enjoyed such pretty things.[1]

The parish priest, or 'Prior', had told Lucia's mother to let her go to the Cova on June 13 but to bring her to him afterwards. Ti Marto heard of this and went first on his own account. The priest said he was sick and tired of the whole thing—everyone seemed to know more about it than he did. Ti Marto could bring his children, or not, as he pleased. Ti Marto ended by saying, with his usual mixture of respect and independence, that he would bring the children because he thought it was the right thing to do, and not to make trouble.

Next day, Maria Rosa in fact brought the two girls, and (Ti Marto thinks) Francisco. Jacinta could not say a word: the priest told her to sit down or run away if she liked. She sat down and began to say her beads. Lucia spoke up well but at times Jacinta would stand up and tell her to answer properly. Fr. Ferreira

---

[1] I cannot find for certain when, or why, the children announced that they had been told a secret. But they certainly believed that they had been told one and never either denied or revealed it. Anyhow, the June experience did not contain *the* secret.

was annoyed and said: 'When I was asking you, you
wouldn't say a word. Now it's the other way round.'
He was genuinely puzzled: our Lady, he considered,
doesn't appear just to tell people to say the rosary
daily—the practice was fairly common in his parish.
Also our Lord usually tells favoured souls to relate
what He says to their confessors or parish priest. This
might be a trick of the devil.

This notion terrified Lucia. Jacinta consoled her
—the devil was ugly and lived underground in hell;
the beautiful Lady went up to heaven. All the same,
Lucia grew dull and apathetic. Wouldn't it be better
to finish it all by saying she *had* told lies? It was
Jacinta and Francisco who told her that *that* would
be a lie; and the poor Lucia dreamed that the devil
had nearly cheated her into sinning and woke up in a
panic. The only grown-up who helped her at all was
Maria Carreira, who came devoutly to the Cova,
took away stones so as to make a little clearing round
the tree, and hung ribbons on it.

But Lucia's depression remained. The priest dis-
believed in the whole thing and his authority was
great. Maria Rosa was sure it was the devil. On
July 12 Lucia told the two others that she would not
go to the Cova. They said they would go anyhow.
Jacinta began to cry. 'If the Lady asks for me', said
Lucia, 'tell her I'm not there because I'm afraid it's
the devil.' Then she went and hid—people were
already coming from everywhere and asking to see her.

Next day, when it was almost time to start, Lucia
felt she must go after all. She went to her cousins'
house and found them kneeling by their beds in tears
because she wasn't coming. So off they went through
roads already thronged. Olimpia, nervous lest the
children should be killed, ran to Maria Rosa's, who
agreed to come—they kilted their over-skirts over

their heads so as not to be recognised. They each took a blessed candle and matches lest some evil thing should befall: then they hid as best they could. But Ti Marto, who was by now a believer, went openly and got as near to the tree as he could. 'If anyone', he had said to Maria Rosa, 'says that we parents are responsible, no one knows better than you and I that we are not.'

At the Cova, the crowd was now dense, but two men were protecting the children from being crushed. They recognised Ti Marto and pulled him close to Jacinta. Lucia was near by, saying her rosary, which all were answering. Suddenly she said: 'Shut your umbrellas!' (for the heat was torrid): 'the Lady is coming.' Ti Marto says that he saw a little greyish cloud on the *azinheira:* the sun's heat lessened: the people became silent. Then it was that Ti Marto heard 'a sound, a little sound, like the buzzing of a horsefly in a bottle. I think talking on the telephone must be like that, though I've never done it. "What is it?" I said to myself. "Is it near or far?" All this was a great proof for me of the miracle.'

Lucia seemed lost in ecstasy. Jacinta said to her: 'Lucia—speak! Our Lady is speaking to you.'

Lucia said again: 'What do you want of me?'

The Lady said: 'I want you to come here again on the 13th of next month. Continue to say the rosary every day in honour of Our Lady of the Rosary to obtain the peace of the world and the end of the war, because only she can obtain it.'

Lucia said: 'I would like to ask who you are and if you will do a miracle so that everyone will believe that you appeared to us.'

'Come here every month and in October I will say who I am and what I want. And I will do a miracle such that all who see it may believe.'

Lucia thereupon made various petitions that had been entrusted to her. The Lady said that she would cure some but not others: that she would not cure Maria Carreira's crippled son nor relieve him of his poverty [he is now 'sacristan' of the shrine]: that a sick person who had asked to be taken to heaven 'soon' must not be in a hurry: 'I know very well when I will come to fetch her.'

'At this moment', says Ti Marto, 'Lucia took a deep breath, went pale as death, and we heard her cry out in terror to our Lady, calling her by her name.'[1]

After a few moments, Lucia said: 'Do you want anything more?'

'No; today there is nothing more.'

Ti Marto says: 'There was a sort of thunder-clap and the little arch which had been put up [over the *azinheira*] to hang the two lanterns on shook as if in an earthquake. Lucia got up off her knees so quickly that her skirts blew out all round her, and pointing to the sky she cried: "There she goes! there she goes!" And then: "Now you can't see her any more." And this too was for me a great proof. The little cloud over the tree melted away.'

People at once thronged round the children. 'Lucia—what did our Lady say to you?'

'It's a secret.'

'Is it a good one?'

'Good for some; but for others, bad.'

'Can't you tell us?'

'No, I can't.'

The crowds were suffocating the children. Ti Marto, suddenly red with rage, perspiring in floods,

[1] I recall that I am writing here only what could be known at the time and can be checked so far as possible by others, and quoting the children when I can. See below, page 158.

forced his way through the crowds with his elbows, picked up his Jacinta, covered her head with his hat and got her away to the road. Olimpia and Maria Rosa, from their hiding-place, were terrified by the shouting in the Cova and thought their children were being killed: then they saw Jacinta safe, and Francisco being carried by someone else, and Lucia in the arms of a certain Carlos Mendes—'Oh Maria Rosa!' cried Olimpia, 'what an enormous man'! Dr. Mendes now thinks that it was really in September that he thus rescued Lucia.

Visits now became a real persecution. The visitors were some of them adulatory; all were inquisitive: they tempted the children with all sorts of gifts to tell the secret: many of them mocked at these simple folks who could not read or write. But as for the secret, says Ti Marto, 'you could not have got it out of them with a corkscrew'. When grand cars were seen to be approaching, the children ran to hide—once, Lucia got under a bed, Francisco, up to an attic. Jacinta was caught, but took refuge in the silence that was so easy for her. Afterwards, the children laughed and danced, enchanted by their escape. . . .

The clergy were, in their way, the most alarming of any because they probed much deeper and kept going back to the beginning. Lucia was to astound Fr. Jongen by saying they didn't like going to the church—they didn't like the priest because he regarded them as liars. There was, however, another priest whose name is not given but who was kind and said to Lucia: 'You must love our Lord very much for all the graces He is giving you.' This became a prayer and she taught it to the other two; it became a favourite with Jacinta especially. Fr. Cruz also visited them, and they took him to Cova da Iria, mounted on a donkey so small that his legs almost touched the ground on either side. He too taught them brief prayers.

But none of this softened her family's feelings towards Lucia—in a way, no wonder, for the Cova, which had supplied them with much of their food, was now trampled all over by visitors and their animals: it was impossible either to sow or to reap. 'If you want something to eat', said Maria Rosa, 'you had better ask our Lady.'

'*You* can have', said her sisters, 'what comes from the Cova.'

As for these sisters, they could no longer sew or weave because of the invasion of visitors, and they had to sell the sheep for next to nothing to anyone who would take them to pasture.

There were, too, accusations of taking money— Lucia had been seen accepting a ten-centavo piece. She said it was only five: her mother beat her really hard for lying. Then it turned out that it was to Jacinta that the little coin had been given, and she took it to Olimpia. 'But by then', says Maria dos Anjos, 'not even St. Anthony could take away Lucia's bruises.' And other women were just as harsh. Olimpia Marto was kinder, but even she used sometimes to slap Jacinta. 'They all go to the Cova because of you!'

'We don't ask them to go', said the child. 'If they want to go, they can go: if they don't, they can stay at home.'

Moreover, all Portugal by now knew about these events: the priests—nay, the Jesuits—were responsible: fraud; money-making; collective hallucination; reactionary propaganda—all the clichés were bandied about. It was a good advertisement.

## CHAPTER 3

# ADMINISTRATIVE ZEAL AND ITS AFTERMATH

TO understand the fantastic episode that follows, we must recall very briefly the disgraceful conduct of Portuguese affairs from 1910 when the Republic was deliriously proclaimed and the Coimbra students nobly rose to the occasion, smashed up the lecture halls, tore up the theologians' robes, and hacked at the portraits of kings. In sixteen years, that is, up to Marshal Gomes da Costa's *coup d'état* on May 28, 1926, there had been at least sixteen 'revolutions', most of them bloodthirsty—the worst was that in October, 1921, the 'revolt of the white ants'—communist-anarchists—and forty-five changes of government. (In Spain, during the fifty-seven months of the Republic's life, there had been twenty-eight such changes, an average of under two months' life per government.)

In October, 1910, the Provisional Government of the Republic suppressed the religious orders and expelled the Jesuits: on the 18th, the religious oath was abolished in the courts of justice, and on the 25th the traditional oath for professors and students by which they had promised to defend the Immaculate Conception. Three days later, holy days were secularised: on November 3, divorce was recognised for the first time in Portuguese history; on the 14th theology was no more to be taught in the University of Coimbra. On Christmas Day marriage was declared a purely civil contract, and on the last day of the year such priests as had received permission to stay in Portugal were forbidden to preach or wear ecclesiastical dress.

On April 20, 1911, came the law of Separation between Church and State: the Church was ruined: monasteries and other such institutions were used as barracks, stables or government buildings. Magahaes Lima, grand-master of the freemasons, said that within a few years no one in Portugal would wish to become a priest: though somewhat later, in Paris, he had to say that the religious question was agitating Portugal as much as ever. The Minister of Justice, Afonso Costa, said that the Catholic religion, main cause of the wretched state of the people, could be eliminated in two generations. When the First World War broke out, the country went from bad to worse: financial ruin was imminent.[1]

The 'Administrator' of the district to which Fatima belonged—Vila Nova de Ourém—was called Artur Santos, a metal-worker, familiarly called 'The Tinker'. He had always concerned himself with politics, and had edited a local journal, the *Ouriense*, in which he aired anti-monarchical and anti-clerical views. When the Republic was declared (1910) he was twenty-six, was elected to the masonic lodge of Leiria, founded another lodge at Vila Nova itself, and became Administrator (I retain this word: 'mayor' seems to me rather too grandiloquent) till 1918. A photograph shows him as a smart and supercilious young man. He was afterwards injured when preparing a bomb to throw at someone he disliked; I cannot find out what ultimately became of

---

[1] See the relevant chapters in Mr. F. C. C. Egerton's *Salazar, Rebuilder of Portugal* (London, 1943). He does not eliminate the shadows; and Portugal is still just escaping the even darker ones that are being cast all over Europe.

him. I am seriously assured that he named his children Republic, Democracy and Liberty. He succeeded in making himself feared as well as detested by the whole countryside, since he acquired other civic positions which gave him a real power.

This man now summoned Abóbora, Ti Marto and the children to his presence. Ti Marto says that Antonio and Lucia arrived at his house during breakfast. All were to be at the Ourém town hall at noon. Lucia asked if Jacinta and Francisco were coming. Certainly not! Ti Marto would answer for them. Lucia ran to Jacinta's room and Jacinta was heard crying: 'If they kill you, tell them that Francisco and I are the same as you and want to be killed too.' On the way, Abóbora went so fast that Lucia fell off her donkey three times. Ti Marto caught them up already in the square. But the town hall was shut. They waited and tried again. At last a man said that the Administrator did not operate there any more and at last they discovered where his office was.

He said at once: 'Where's the child?'

Ti Marto saw that he did not even know that three children were involved.

He said: 'It's over three leagues from here to our village; the children can't walk all that way and they aren't used to the donkey.' He just stopped himself adding 'And that children of that age should be called up!'

Santos was annoyed, and tried to make Lucia reveal the secret, but not a word. He asked Abóbora if they believed such things in Fatima. Abóbora said, No: they thought them old wives' tales.

But Ti Marto said: 'Here am I, and my children say the same as I do.'

'So *you* believe it?'

'Yes, I believe what they say.'

There were some journalists present, who all laughed. Santos continued to threaten Lucia that he would kill her if she did not reveal the secret.

Ti Marto said: 'If you send for us, we shall have to come as often as you please. But kindly remember that we've got to live.'

This did not mean that Santos had abdicated. On August 13, Ti Marto was sent for to return at once from a plot of land where he had begun to work. Naturally, since it was the 13th, there were a lot of people about; but what first struck Ti Marto as odd was that he found his wife sitting in the kitchen, very upset. Ti Marto continues with his incomparable naïf realism that he refused to hurry but went and washed his hands and took the towel into the sitting-room drying his hands as he went. There he saw the Administrator but 'wasn't very polite to him' because there was a priest there too with whom he shook hands first. Then he said to Santos that he hadn't expected to see him here.

Santos said: 'No. After all, I thought I'd like to see the miracle. We'll go together and I'll take the children in my carriage. We'll see and believe, like St. Thomas.'

'I could see', said Ti Marto, 'that he was nervous because he kept looking all around.'

Santos said it was getting late—they had better call the children. Ti Marto said they would be ready when it was time to go. Just then they all came in. They said it wasn't necessary to go in the carriage. Santos said it would be better—they would be there in a moment and no one would bother them. Ti Marto insisted that they could go alone.

'Then we'll go to Fatima', said Santos. 'I've got something I want to ask the parish priest.'

When they got to the presbytery, Santos shouted: 'Bring the first!'

'The first what?' said Marto.

'Lucia', Santos answered.

Lucia went in and the priest heckled her, I confess, very roughly. 'Those who go about spreading such lies as you do will be judged and go to hell. . . . More and more people are being deceived by you . . .' and so forth.

'These are supernatural things', said Santos. 'Let us go.' And he put the children into his carriage under the eyes of their parents. The horse was whipped up and it went off like a flash, allegedly towards the Cova.

But after a while Lucia said: 'This isn't the way.' Santos said he wanted to go first to Ourém and see the priest. They would come back by motor-car to the Cova in plenty of time. But people, streaming towards the Cova, began to recognise the carriage and the children, so he covered them with rugs and thus they arrived at his house. He locked them up in a room, saying they would not come out till they had told the secret. 'If they kill us', said Jacinta, 'we shall go straight to heaven.' However, Santos's wife, a kindly soul, brought them a meal and toys, and actually called them to play with her own children.

Meanwhile the possibility of the Apparitions being diabolic in origin had caused stories to circulate, such as that the devil was only waiting to get enough people there to make the ground open and swallow them all up. They came, however, in still greater numbers. At about 11, Maria dos Anjos arrived with some candles, but not the children. Then someone said that Santos had kidnapped them. An uproar arose, and, says Maria Carreira (on whom we chiefly rely for this episode), anything might have happened had not the 'clap of thunder' occurred just then. Some thought it sounded from the road; others, from the tree: Maria thought it came from very far away. They then saw a small cloud, very diaphanous and white, rest for a moment on the tree and then rise and disappear. And then they noticed 'what we had seen before [I do not know when] and were to see in the following months. Our faces were reflecting all the colours of the rainbow, pink, red, blue . . . the trees seemed made not of leaves but of flowers, each leaf a flower. The ground came out in colours and so did our clothes. The lanterns on the arch seemed like gold.'

When all this died away, everyone began shouting that they must go off to Fatima—shouting against the priest, against the Administrator—the noise could be heard even in Aljustrel. Ti Marto, who had come to the Cova, did his best to quiet the clamour, but in vain. He returned home to find Olimpia in tears. She herself had been to Fatima and then ran back to Maria Rosa:

'What will become of us? They have taken our children.'

Maria Rosa seemed almost more pleased than distressed:

'If they are lying, it'll teach them a lesson. If they aren't, our Lady will see to them.'

'You've got only one', said Olimpia, 'but we have our two—and such babies!' And she continued to weep.

Fr. Ferreira was so alarmed by all this that he wrote to the Lisbon paper *Ordem* and to the *Ouriense* a vehement defence of his attitude. I quote only parts of it because it is full of repetitions:

'To believers and unbelievers! Reluctantly, as a Catholic priest, I beg to make known the following before all who may hear rumours—infamous and damaging to my reputation as parish priest—that I was an accomplice in the imprisonment of three children in my parish who affirm that they have seen our Lady. I make this statement on the authority of their parents and for the satisfaction of the five to six thousand persons who came many miles and at great sacrifice to see and speak with them. I deny this infamous and insidious calumny and declare before the whole world that I had nothing whatever to do, directly or indirectly, with this impious and sacrilegious act.' (He then says that the Administrator had not told him what he was going to do. Santos had first examined them at home and had then brought them to the presbytery. Then he drove them away to Vila Nova de Ourém.) 'Why did he choose my house from which to act? In order to escape the consequences of his action? In order that the people should riot, as they did, and accuse me of complicity? Or for some other reason? I do not know. I decline all responsibility in the matter and leave judgement to God.' Then he very interestingly says that 'thousands of eyewitnesses can attest that the presence of the children was not necessary for the Queen of Heaven to manifest her power. They will witness to the extraordinary phenomena which occurred to confirm their faith. By now it is not a trio of children but thousands of all ages and conditions who have seen for themselves. If my absence from the Cova gave offence to believers, my presence would have been no less objectionable to unbelievers. The Blessed Virgin has no need of the parish-priest in order to manifest her goodness, and the enemies of religion need not tarnish their benevolence by attributing the faith of the people to the presence or absence of the priest. Faith is the gift of God and not of priests. That is the true motive of my absence and apparent indifference to so sublime and marvellous an event. This is why I have not replied to the thousand questions and letters that have been addressed to me.'

He adds that he will not offer his own narrative
of those events because the press will doubtless have
given its own. I presume that his rather startling
change of attitude was due to his hearing about the
coloured lights and the sounds, as well as fear for his
own safety; it remains remarkable that the republican
press should have published so militant a letter.

Next day, at Ourém, the children were interrogated, first, by an old woman, and then, about 10
o'clock, by Santos, who alternately threatened them
and tried to bribe them with money and a gold chain.
Senhora Santos again gave them a good lunch; but
after further interrogations they were put into the
public gaol and told they would be brought out only
to be put into a cauldron of boiling oil and fried to
death. Jacinta cried bitterly at the thought of dying
without seeing her mother again. The others did their
best to console her; and indeed their fellow-prisoners,
who were of a very different type, but kind-hearted
Portuguese all the same, kept trying to cheer her up
by saying that after all they had only to tell the
secret and all would be well. One of the prisoners
had a concertina and began to play tunes and in a
moment or two all of them were dancing. Jacinta
knew how to dance the fandango, and soon enough
the small child found herself literally whirled through
the air by her stalwart partner. But after a while she
asked him to put her down and to hang a medal that
she had upon a nail. The three children knelt down
and began the rosary. Soon the others were saying it
too. One man kept his hat on. 'When you pray',
said Francisco, 'you should take your hat off.'

The man, irritated, threw it down: Francisco put
it on a bench.

On to this unexpected scene a guard suddenly
entered and ordered the children out. At all costs

they must be made to tell the secret: the boiling oil
awaited them if they refused. They remained dumb.
Jacinta, trembling but resolute, was marched off.
Francisco took out his rosary and said a Hail Mary.
The guard asked what he was doing. 'I am saying an
*Ave* so that Jacinta may not be afraid.' The door
opened. A second guard came in: Jacinta was dead:
it was her brother's turn. He too was removed and
Lucia was left alone. We have to remember that these
children really believed that what had been threatened
would be carried out: we need not dwell on their
amazing heroism. However, when Lucia in her turn
was summoned, she found the others alive and safe,
not having said one word about the secret. There
was one more threat that they would all be put into
the oil together, but the night passed, the feast of the
Assumption dawned, and the Administrator, defeated,
drove the children off to the presbytery at Fatima.

Despite the almost unbelievably ignoble behaviour
of Santos, perhaps we ought to do him the justice of
imagining that he really did think the 'secret' had
some political or anti-republican content: any
'clerical' demonstration might be taken as masking a
plot: tyrants are always stupidly self-confident or
superstitiously afraid. Anyhow, by concentrating on
the 'secret' Santos was shutting his eyes to what was
happening at Cova da Iria. The Mass of the Assumption was hardly over when Ti Marto began to be
questioned, but the last he had heard was that the
children had been seen playing under the verandah
of the Administrator's house. But at that very moment
they were seen outside the presbytery. 'I hardly
knew how I got there . . . but I rushed up and hugged
my Jacinta. I picked her up and even now I remember
how I put her on my right arm.' (Women carried
their children on the left arm so as to leave the right

arm free.) Lucia and Francisco also rushed up and begged him to bless them.

'Just then', says Ti Marto, 'there appeared a funny little official in the service of the Administrator; he shook and trembled in the oddest way: I have never seen anything like it. He said: "Well, here are your children." I burst out: "This might have come to a bad end and it's not your fault that it didn't. You wanted them to say that they were lying and you couldn't. And even if you'd made them, I'd have told the truth." ' The priest came running out of the church prepared to rebuke Ti Marto who, he thought, was causing the uproar. 'But I knew how to answer him too. . . .' Then Marto quieted the crowd, saying: 'It all comes from lack of faith and is allowed by God.' Whereupon Santos appeared and said: 'That's enough, Senhor Marto!' Marto appeased him too and was called by him into the presbytery, saying: 'I prefer Senhor Abóbora's conversation but I must see Marto too.' Fr. Ferreira said: 'Senhor Administrator, we cannot do without religion.'

Santos asked Marto to come and have a glass of wine with him. Marto was for refusing, when he saw a crowd of lads armed with sticks and that Santos was really nervous, so he changed his mind and accepted. As they went down the steps, Santos said: 'Be sure I treated the children well.' 'That's all right Senhor', said Marto: 'it's not I but the people who want to know that.' They went to the inn and Santos ordered wine and bread and cheese and 'started a silly conversation in which I took no interest whatsoever; but at a certain point he tried to make me think that the children had told him the secret. I said without moving a muscle: "Right! right! Since they wouldn't tell it to their father and mother, it's only natural they should tell it to you." '

Ti Marto had to go to the post. Santos therefore added to his exhibition of good will by giving him a lift. People said: 'Ti Marto's talked too much: the Tinker's taking him to gaol!'

Meanwhile Maria Carreira was in a difficulty. She had put a little table in front of the *azinheira* with candles and flowers. People began to put money too upon it; on the day when the children were kidnapped and the colours in the sky appeared, money simply 'poured in': people pushed so hard that it looked as if they would upset it all. They shouted to her to take it and not to lose any. She put it into her lunch-bag and it was very heavy. (The older heavier coinage was in use.) Later that day she saw Olimpia's eldest son and called to him to ask what she should do. He would make no suggestion. She took it home and counted it. On the 14th she went to Ti Marto's and found Maria Rosa and Fr. Ferreira there. She went straight up to Ti Marto, but he refused to touch it. Maria Rosa refused it quite angrily. So did the priest. 'There might have been a curse upon it!' Maria Carreira in her turn got angry—'the mustard was up *her* nose too'—and said she would put it back where she found it. The priest told her not to do that, but to keep it or give it to someone else until they saw what came of all this. Later, four men arrived and asked for the money and said they would build a chapel. She in her turn refused to give it to them, consulted Fr. Ferreira and was told that she had done right, and that anyhow he would not have anything to do with the affair.

On Sunday, August 19, she saw Lucia's father after Mass: she had been told to beware of him as he had often had too much to drink and was angry with her for going to his property in the Cova. She rather timidly apologised if she had been trespassing and asked his permission to go there. He was sober but pretty rough: 'Put as many flowers there as you like; but I won't have tabernacles on my land. Someone told me', he added, 'that you took away a lot of money from my land; but I don't want it.' 'Nor do I', said Maria. Then she thought she might use it as stipends for Masses for those who had put it there. Then she suddenly thought of asking Lucia who said she would ask our Lady on the 13th of the next month. But her opportunity came earlier. . . .

In the afternoon of Sunday, August 19, it was time for the sheep to be taken out to pasture. Jacinta had been called to help her mother, and Lucia went off with Francisco and his elder brother João. They went to a place called Valinhos, belonging to one of Lucia's uncles. At about 4 o'clock, they noticed that the air grew cooler; the sunlight dimmed somewhat and there was the 'flash of lightning'. Interestingly enough, Lucia's sister Teresa and her husband were just entering Fatima when the air cooled, the sunlight looked yellowish and then took on various colours as it had done at the Cova. 'What is this?' she exclaimed, 'another mystery!' For the same colours began to show on her husband's white shirt. 'How mistaken we've all been!' 'Why?' said he. 'Don't you see that it's all like the 13th?' When they reached the church, the colours faded out. It turned out to be just the same time as what was happening at Valinhos.[1]

Lucia, on her side, was distressed. The Lady must be coming, but Jacinta wasn't there. She told João to run and fetch her, but he wanted to see the Lady for himself. Lucia had a little money and she gave it to him—there would be more when he came back. He

[1] What did Teresa mean by their having been 'mistaken'? This was not a '13th', so the colours after all had no connection with the apparitions.

gave his message: 'What's all this nonsense?' said Olimpia. 'Must the priest always have his sacristan?' In the end she gave way: João found his sister at her god-mother's and they ran hand in hand to Valinhos. Olimpia too went off to see what she could but arrived too late; and as for João, he saw nothing at all.

The moment Jacinta appeared, there was a second flash, and lo, the Lady, again above a tree but a larger one. Lucia as usual asked what she wished, and again was told to return to the Cova on the 13th and to say the rosary daily. Lucia once more asked for a miracle so that all might believe.

'I will grant one in October, but not so grand a one as if they had not taken you to the Town. St. Joseph too will come with the holy Child to bring peace to the world. Our Lord will also come to bless the people. Our Lady of the Rosary and Our Lady of Sorrows will come too.'

Lucia then asked what was to be done with the offerings at the Cova. The Lady said that they were to make two portable stands (andores): Lucia, with three other little girls in white, was to carry one; Francisco, with three other little boys also in white, would carry the other. The money for the andores was for the feast of Our Lady of the Rosary.[1]

Lucia related (I am not sure when) that the Lady repeated that they were to pray very much and make sacrifices for sinners because many souls went to hell because no one made sacrifices for them.

[1] Maria Carreira said she was sorry the money could not be used for building a chapel. Lucia agreed, but said they must do as the Lady ordered. When, therefore, in her document of December 8, 1941, she wrote that our Lady did say that extra money could be used for a chapel, it is recognised that she was confusing this apparition with that in September. This is in harmony with what she said to the parish priest two days later (August 21, 1917) and with the canonical enquiry (July 8, 1924).

Francisco and Jacinta went home carrying sprays of the tree over which our Lady stood. Maria dos Anjos says that Jacinta rushed up to Maria Rosa, who with others was there at her house-door, and cried that they had seen our Lady at the Valinhos.

'When will these lies cease?' she said. 'Now you will be seeing our Lady all over the place!'

Jacinta gave her the two sprays saying that our Lady had put one foot on the first, the other on the second. Maria Rosa perceived that they smelt very sweet—not like roses—like what? she could not tell. She put them on the table till someone could say what they smelt like. Jacinta, however, secretly made off with them to show them to her parents: it would seem that as from that time Lucia began to be treated more kindly in her home.

Ti Marto came back later. A man said to him: 'The miracle's going well!'

'What do you mean? I know nothing new.'

'Our Lady's appeared again to your two and to Abóbora's girl. I tell you, your Jacinta's got something special about her. She hadn't gone with the others and it was only when she came that our Lady appeared.'

Ti Marto went out into the yard to think this over, and then into the kitchen. Jacinta came in looking radiant with a branch 'about this size', says Marto, in her hand. 'As she came in I smelt a most delicious scent that I can't describe. I put out my hand to take the branch and said: "What have you got there?" "It's the branch our Lady stood on." I took the branch and smelt it, but the scent had gone.'

CHAPTER 4

## SEPTEMBER TO OCTOBER 12

IF the people of Aljustrel, and in particular the
parish priest and most of the children's families,
remained incredulous, we have scriptural warrant
for not being surprised. But the crowds that came
from elsewhere constantly increased till on September
13 the whole area was thronged. There were, probably
for the first time, some priests and seminarians. There
may have been some thirty of the latter, for the long
vacation was ending and they did not want to return
to their seminaries without having seen what was
happening. They went jumping from rock to rock,
climbing walls and stiles, till a priest warned them
that the whole thing might be of diabolic origin
or a fiasco. They went and stood for a while where
the basilica now is, but gradually worked their way
down as near as they could to the *azinheira* tree.

Among the priests were Mgr. J. Quaresma, Vicar
General of Leiria, Mgr. Gois, and Canon Formigão.
Fifteen years later, Mgr. Quaresma wrote to Mgr.
Gois recalling their doubts and hesitations before
leaving Leiria in a rickety old carriage and how Fr.
Gois found a place dominating the whole scene. At
midday there was silence save for the murmur of
prayers. Suddenly, he writes, there were 'cries of
jubilation and voices praising the Blessed Virgin'.
Arms were raised pointing to the sky—'Look, don't
you see?' 'Yes, I do!' Mgr. Quaresma also looked into
the cloudless blue sky:

'With great astonishment I saw, clearly and
distinctly, a luminous globe moving from east to west,
gliding slowly and majestically through space. My

60

friend also looked and had the good fortune to enjoy the same unexpected and delightful vision. Suddenly the globe with its extraordinary light disappeared. Near us was a little girl dressed like Lucia and about the same age who continued to cry happily: "I still see it! I still see it! Now it's coming down." After a few minutes she began to exclaim again, pointing to the sky: "Now it's going up again", and she followed the globe with her eyes till it disappeared in the direction of the sun.'

Mgr. Quaresma asked his companion what he thought of it, and he answered: 'That it was our Lady.' Quaresma was sure that the children had seen our Lady herself, and they, 'the means of transport—if one may so express it—which brought her from heaven to the inhospitable wastes of the Serra de Aire'.

He then writes: 'I must emphasise that all those around us appeared to have seen the same thing, for one heard cries of joy and praises of our Lady. But some saw nothing. Near us was a simple devout creature crying bitterly because she had seen nothing.'

They went from group to group in the Cova and again on the way home questioning all kinds of people, 'but one and all affirmed the reality of the phenomena that we ourselves had witnessed'.

These slight contradictions in writing—'all saw the same . . . some saw nothing . . .' will always be noticeable as we proceed. Some also were aware of the freshening of the atmosphere, the paling of the sun 'till the stars could be seen' (I doubt if this is mentioned elsewhere) and a kind of rain of flower-petals which vanished before reaching the earth (this last phenomenon was recurrent and we consider it later).

Lucia wrote afterwards of the enthusiasm of the enormous throngs, of the way people fell on their knees as the children passed, calling out all sorts of petitions, or climbed trees to see them.

When the Apparition came, Lucia asked, just as always: 'What do you want of me?' And the Lady repeated all that she had said last time—they must say the rosary daily in honour of Our Lady of the Rosary to obtain the end of the war; that St. Joseph and the Holy Child would appear to give peace to the world; that our Lord would bless the people, and that they would see the 'forms' of Our Lady of Sorrows and of Carmel.

Lucia set forth her petitions: the Lady repeated that she would grant some, others not.

Lucia said: 'The people would much like to build a chapel here.' The Lady said they should use half the money received up to date for the two 'litters' and place Our Lady of the Rosary on the one —it is not said what should be on the other and there seems to be no record of the actual making or using of these 'litters'—while the other half could be used to help to build a chapel.

'Many people say I am a liar', said Lucia, 'and deserve to be hanged or burnt. Please work a miracle so that all may believe.'

The Lady again said that she would.

'Some people have given me two letters and a bottle of eau de Cologne for Your Ladyship.'

'That is of no use in heaven', said she, and disappeared.

We mentioned, as among the priests present at Cova da Iria on September 13, Canon Manuel Formigão, professor at the seminary and lyceum of Santarém. Of all the phenomena alluded to he noticed only the lessening of the sunlight which he thought might naturally occur at that altitude. But the demeanour of the children had so deeply impressed him that on September 27 he returned to question them quietly. He records his first interrogatory, which was with Francisco, as follows:

'What did you see at Cova da Iria these last months?'

'I saw our Lady.'

'Where does she appear?'

'On the top of a *carrasqueira*.'

'Does she appear suddenly, or do you see her coming from somewhere?'

'I see her coming from the side where the sun rises and place herself on the *carrasqueira*.'

'Does she come slowly or quickly?'

'She always comes quickly.'

'Do you hear what she says to Lucia?'

'No.'

'Do you ever speak to the Lady? Does she ever speak to you?'

'No; I have never asked her anything: she speaks only to Lucia.'

'At whom does she look? also at you and a Jacinta or only at Lucia?'

'She looks at all three of us but longer at Lucia.'

'Does she ever cry or smile?'

'Neither the one or the other. She is always grave (*seria*).'

'How is she dressed?'

'She has a long dress and over it a veil [1] which covers her head and falls to the edges of her dress.'

'What colour are the dress and the veil?'

'White, and the dress has gold lines.'

'What is her attitude?'

'Like someone praying. She has her hands at the height of her breast.'

[1] This word—*manto*—is usually translated 'mantle', but this suggests to me something placed over the shoulders, so I venture to say 'veil'.

'Does she hold anything in her hands?'

'She carries a rosary round the palm and the back of her right hand. It hangs down over her dress.'

'What has she got in her ears?'

'You don't see her ears because they are covered with the veil.'

'What colour is the rosary?'

'White too.'

'Is the Lady beautiful?'

'Yes, she is.'

'More than that little girl over there?'

'More beautiful than anyone I have seen.'

Jacinta was brought in next—she was playing with other children in the road: the Canon sat her down beside him and asked his questions. I do not transcribe these when they are identical with the previous ones unless her answer adds or emphasises something. She said that the white dress was 'adorned' with gold; that you could not see the Lady's hair or ears, for they were covered by the veil: her hands were joined with the fingers pointing up. At first she said that the rosary was in the Lady's right hand, but when the Canon insisted, she became confused (after all, the Lady's right was to Jacinta's left), and he did not dwell on this.

'What was the chief thing that the Lady told Lucia?'

'That we were to say the rosary every day.'

'And do you?'

'Yes, every day, with Francisco and Lucia.'

After half an hour Lucia arrived: she had been helping with the vintage. The Canon thought she looked better nourished than the others and had a cleaner skin and colour. She was quite without self-consciousness, whereas Jacinta had been very shy. She gave no signs of vanity or confusion. But she was visibly tired and depressed, doubtless owing to the endless questionings to which she had been subjected. After saying that our Lady had appeared five times, always on the 13th except in August, when she came to the Valinhos on the 9th, she was asked:

'People say that our Lady appeared to you also last year. Is there any truth in that?'

'She never appeared to me last year—never before May this year. I never said so to anyone, because it is not true.'

'Where does she come from? from the east?'

'I don't know. I don't see her come from anywhere. She appears over the *azinheira* and when she goes away she goes into the sky where the sun rises.'

'How long does she stay? A long time, or short?'

'Short.'

'Enough to say an Our Father and Hail Mary, or more?'

'A good deal more, but not always the same time. Perhaps it would not be long enough to say a rosary (five decades).'

'The first time you saw her were you frightened?'

'I was, so much so that I wanted to run away with Jacinta and Francisco but she said we must not be afraid because she would not hurt us. She wore a white dress coming down to her feet and her head is covered by a veil of the same colour and length.'

'Has the dress anything on it?'

'You see, in front, two gold cords that come down from the neck and are joined at the waist by a tassel, also gold.'

'Has she a sash or girdle?'

'No.'

'Has she rings in her ears?'

'Little gold rings.'

(Lucia did not notice if the rosary were of fifteen or five decades: beads, cross and chain were, all of them, white.)

'Did you ever ask her who she was?'

'I asked, but she said she would tell us only on October 13.'

'Did you ask her where she came from?'

'I did, and she answered that she came from heaven.'

'When did you ask her this?'

'The second time—the 13th of June.'

'Did she sometimes smile or was she sad?'

'She neither smiled nor was sad. She was always grave.'

'Did she tell you or your cousins to say certain prayers?'

'She told us to say the rosary in honour of Our Lady of the Rosary to obtain peace for the world.'

'Did she say that many people should be present during apparitions at the Cova da Iria?'

'She said nothing about that.'

'Is it true that she told you a secret that you were not to tell to anyone whomsoever?'

'That is true.'

'Does it concern you or your cousins also?'

'All three.'

'Couldn't you tell it even to your confessor?'

(Lucia seemed confused and the Canon did not press the question.)

'In order to get freed by the Administrator, did you tell him something as if it were the secret, thus tricking him, and boast of it afterwards?'

'That is not true. Senhor Santos really did wish me to reveal the secret but I could not and did not though he tried to make me do what he wanted in every way. I told him everything the Lady had said to me except the secret. Perhaps that is why he thought I had told him the secret too. I never meant to deceive him.'

'Did the Lady tell you to learn to read?'

'Yes; the second time she appeared.'

'But what would be the good of that if she told you she would take you to heaven next October?'

'That is not true. She never told me that she would and I have never told anyone any such things.'

'What did the Lady say should be done with the money that people left at the foot of the *azinheira*?'

'She said that we must spend it on two *andores* and that I and Jacinta and two other girls must carry one and Francisco and three other boys the other to the parish church. Part of the money was to go to the cult and feast of Our Lady of the Rosary and the rest to help to build a new chapel.'

'Where does the Lady want the chapel built? In the Cova?'

'I don't know. The Lady didn't say.'

'Are you very glad that the Lady appeared to you?' 'Yes.'

'Will she come alone on October 13?'

'St. Joseph and the Child will come too, and soon afterwards peace will be granted to the world.'

'Did the Lady reveal anything else?'

'She said that on October 13 she would work a miracle so that people should believe she appeared.'

'Why do you often lower your eyes instead of keeping them on the Lady?'

'Because she sometimes blinds me.'

'Did she teach you a prayer?'

'Yes; she wished us to say it after each mystery of the rosary.'

'Do you know it by heart?'

'Yes—"O my Jesus, forgive us; deliver us from the fire of hell; take all souls to heaven, especially those who are most in need." '

The Canon was profoundly impressed by the sincerity of the children, but he wished to exclude all possible idea of an hallucination. On the eve of October 13 he spent the night with the Gonçalves family, friends of his, at Montelo, about two kilometres from Fatima. Here he questioned Manuel, the eldest son, known to be a man of good sense and power of observation. I need quote only a summary of this conversation. Sr. Gonçalves said that the Marto family was profoundly religious and respected by all. Lucia's father was not often at church, but a good fellow. On June 13 some of his friends had made him drunk hoping that he would do something silly at the Cova. He allowed Lucia to go, but ordered the other people off his property. Someone pushed him and he fell over, so no one paid any attention. At first, nobody had believed the children, but gradually a good proportion believed (as Gonçalves did himself) that they were telling the truth. 'Signs' were numerous —nearly everyone saw them. Both in July and August a cloud seemed to come down on the tree—not a 'dust-cloud': there was no dust. In August, white clouds near the sun turned blood-red, pink and yellow —the people themselves turned yellow. The sunlight waned; and in July and August a 'noise' was heard. A hoax was quite impossible. People often offered the children gifts—if these were pressed on them, they accepted, but reluctantly. The families are 'comfortable'. If Abóbora is not better off, it is his own fault. When Lucia speaks to the Lady she speaks loudly, some say they have heard the answers. People come in crowds, especially on Sunday evenings, and especially from outside the parish. They say the rosary and sing hymns.

The Canon then went to Aljustrel: Lucia was helping to repair the roof but came down at once. He makes the following selection of questions and answers. He questioned Maria Rosa first.

'I think you have a book called *Short Mission* which you sometimes read to your children?'

'Yes.'

'Have you ever read about the apparition of La Salette to Lucia or other children?'

'Only to Lucia and my own children.'

'Did she ever speak about it or show that it had made a great impression on her?'

'I don't remember that she ever spoke of it.'

The examination of Lucia was before four reliable witnesses. She repeated what she had said about the *andores;* said that she thought our Lady would like the chapel at the Cova but wasn't sure; and added that our Lady had often said that she would work a miracle, once when Lucia asked her during the first Apparition. (Here is a small slip.)

'Are you not afraid if nothing special happens that day (i.e. October 13)? of what people will do to you?'

'Not at all.'

'Do you feel something inside you which drags you to the Cova on the 13th?'

'I feel I want to go and would be sad if I didn't.'

(The Lady never made the sign of the Cross, nor prayed, nor told her beads, but often told Lucia to pray.)

'Did she tell you to pray for the conversion of sinners?'

'No; she only told me to pray to Our Lady of the Rosary for the end of the war.'

'Did you see signs such as other people say they saw, such as a star or roses detaching themselves from the Lady's dress, etc.?'

'I saw no star or other sign.'—Nor had she heard an earthquake or other noise, nor was she learning to read.

'Then you are not doing what the Lady wants?'

Lucia made no answer—perhaps, it is thought, not to criticise her mother who had asked what it could matter to the Lady whether Lucia could read or not? Lucia proceeded that it was she, not the Lady, who told the people to kneel—she herself sometimes stood and sometimes knelt. The Lady had a sweet voice and seemed about fifteen.

'Is the light that surrounds her very beautiful?'
'More beautiful than the most brilliant sunlight.'
The Lady never greeted her with head or hands
—she never laughed—she never looked at the people.
Lucia herself never heard the people while she was
speaking to the Lady. She remembered her mother
reading about an apparition of our Lady to a girl
but had never thought or talked about it.

The Canon went on to the Martos. If he often
repeated his questions it was presumably to see if
the children could be caught out in contradictions
either with themselves or with one another. He asked
Jacinta if she too heard the secret and if so, when?

'I did. On St. Anthony's feast.'
'Is it that you will be rich?'
'No.'
'That you will be good and happy?'
'Yes; it is for the good of all of us.'
'That you will go to heaven?'
'No.'
'If the people knew the secret, would they be sad?'
'Yes.'
'How did the Lady have her hands?'
'She had them stretched out.'
'Always?'
'Sometimes she turned the palms up to heaven.
. . . She said she wanted us to come six months
running till October when she would tell us what
she wanted.'
'Was there light round her head?'
'Yes.'
'Could you look easily at her face?'
'No, because it hurts my eyes.' Last time she had
not heard everything because of the noise the people
were making.
Francisco said that he was nine; that he never
heard what the Lady said; that she had light round

her head but that he could look only a little because
of the light. Her dress had some 'gold cords'.

'Would the people be sad if they knew the secret?'
'Yes.'


But as October 13 approached, the whole of
Portugal was talking of the promised miracle and
something like panic reigned in the houses of the three
children and indeed in the whole neighbourhood.
There would be bombs—the houses would be destroyed—better lock the children up—better still,
take them right away and hide them. Maria Rosa,
who had been giving Lucia a very bad time, said
that if it was genuinely our Lady she really might
have worked a miracle before then . . . have made a
spring break forth . . . when it rained there was a
mere drop of moisture there, nothing more—'Oh,
where will all this end?'

Maria dos Anjos herself went to the children,
who were by the well, and said: 'Just tell me that
nothing really happened and I will tell Fr. Ferreira,
and he will give it out in church.' Lucia screwed her
forehead up. Jacinta said, 'in her tiny voice', 'Say
it if you like, but we *saw* her.'

Hardly had the 12th dawned when Maria Rosa
woke Lucia up and said they had better go to confession—everyone said they would be killed next day.
Lucia said she would go with her mother if she
wanted her to, but not because she was afraid.

As for the Martos, a Fr. Poças, a neighbouring
parish priest, and one of his parishioners came there,
and when Ti Marto returned and they had all
assembled Fr. Poças attacked the children violently and
said that if they didn't own up to its being nonsense he
would tell everyone so. People believed him, and they
were going to the Cova to destroy everything. Ti

Marto said: 'Very well. Better telegraph that every-where.' The priest said that that was just what he would do, and then no one would come. Ti Marto was very angry, and Jacinta, 'who never liked to see anyone angry', slipped away. Her father said to the priest: 'There's nothing to prevent your doing as you please, but leave my children alone.'

The other visitor said furiously that the whole thing was witchcraft: he had himself had a servant who got some idea into her head and nothing would dislodge it.

They then found Jacinta playing on the doorstep with another child.

'Listen', said Fr. Poças: 'Lucia has told us every-thing, and now we know it's all a lie.'

'Lucia never said that', replied Jacinta firmly.

The man then produced a coin to give to Jacinta.

'You mustn't do that', said Ti Marto.

'Surely I can give something to João, then?'

'You needn't; but you can if you like.'

As they left, the priest said to Ti Marto: 'You played your part very well. Congratulations.'

'Well or ill', said he, 'that's my way. You haven't made them deny their story, and if you had, I'd still believe in them.'

## CHAPTER 5

# OCTOBER 13

THE events of October 13 may be said to fall into three parts—the Apparition itself; the 'atmospheric phenomena', as the Bishop of Leiria was to call them, and the supplementary visions, if I may so name them, seen by the children in the sky.

For days beforehand pilgrims had been making their way to the Cova. Whole villages seemed to have been evacuated. On the day itself, green-decorated wagons, luxurious motor-cars, mule- and donkey-carts and bicycles, as well as throngs of pedestrians were converging on the Cova. The drizzle with which the 13th started turned into a steady downpour: everyone was soaked to the skin. The number usually given for the crowd is 70,000. Professor Garrett of Coimbra University put it much higher than that. And the crowd was by no means of believers only: many had come to mock: many, who were just sceptical, wished that on this awful day they had stayed at home.

I

At Aljustrel, Maria Rosa sincerely thought it was her last day; if Lucia was to die, she would die with her. With infinite difficulty they got through to the Martos' cottage: it was packed with people, climbing on to the furniture, muddying the beds. Olimpia was in tears: Ti Marto had been urged not to go to the Cova—the children might be unharmed, being so small, but not *he!* He professed his faith and said he would certainly go. The two children were completely

unperturbed. A lady had brought a blue dress for
Lucia and a white one for Jacinta and put white
wreaths on their heads.[1] They left the house in the
drenching downpour: people knelt in the mud 'as
though', said Ti Marto, 'my children had the power
of saints'.

At the Cova, a chauffeur picked up Jacinta and
struggled through the crowd, Ti Marto close behind.
Jacinta saw him being hustled to and fro and began
to cry and called out: 'Don't push my father—don't
hurt him!' Lucia and Francisco got through too,
Maria Rosa keeping as near as she could; Olimpia
had got lost.

Very soon the crowd became quiet, but a priest
who had been there all the night asked when the
Lady would come, and the children answering 'at
noon', said, looking at his watch: 'It's noon now: our
Lady doesn't lie.' After a few minutes he said: 'It's
past midday. You see it's all a delusion. Run away
all of you.'[2]

Lucia refused to go and the priest began to push
them. Lucia, on the verge of tears, said: 'If anyone
wants to go, they can. I shall stay where I am. Our
Lady said she would come and she will come this
time too.' Then she said to Jacinta: 'Kneel down.
Our Lady is coming. I see the lightning.'

Maria Rosa, close behind her, and in torment,
said: 'Look closely, my child: make no mistake!'

A sort of mist seemed to surround the tree, or,
some say, the children.

Lucia asked her unvarying question: 'What do
you want of me?'

[1] It is said that they refused the dresses and wore their First Communion dresses. But Jacinta had not yet made her First Communion.
[2] There was a difference of about $1\frac{1}{2}$ hours between sun-time and
the official time.

'I want a chapel to be built here in my honour. I am the Lady of the Rosary. Continue to say the rosary every day. The war is going to end and the soldiers will soon return to their homes.'

'I have many petitions; will you grant them?'

'Some, yes; others, no. People must amend their lives and ask pardon for their sins. They must not offend our Lord any more; He is already much offended.'

'Do you want anything more from me?'

'I want nothing more.'

Lucia cried out: 'There she goes! there she goes!' and then: 'Look at the sun'!

She did not know she said this, nor was she alluding to the 'solar phenomena' about to be described, but to other visions which the children were seeing, in the way proper to each, near the sun: but we postpone the study of these till we reach the enquiry made into them by Canon Formigão.


II


I will now describe, briefly and baldly, what happened after the normal apparition, adding the declarations of eyewitnesses only. The rain stopped abruptly and the sun became visible through a rift in the clouds like a pale disc easily looked at. It then appeared to rotate and shoot out prismatic rays. It then seemed to approach the earth very rapidly, to emit a red glow and a great heat. It then resumed its normal appearance. I will now extract the parts of Canon Formigão's interrogatory, made that same evening, which refer to this. From Lucia he simply asked if she had seen signs in the sun: she said: 'I saw it go round like a wheel.' On this occasion he seems to have asked nothing from the other two. But on the 19th he revisited the children and said to Francisco:

'Did you see signs in the sun? what did you see?'

'I looked and I saw that the sun was going round like a wheel: it seemed like a wheel of fire.'

'What were the colours that you saw in the sun?'

'I saw very pretty colours, blue, yellow and others.'

And to Jacinta: 'Did you look at the sun?'

'Yes.'

'And what did you see?'

'I saw the sun bright red, green and other colours, and I saw it was going round like a wheel.'

'Did you hear Lucia tell the people to look at the sun?'

'I heard her. She said with a very loud voice that I should look at the sun. It was already going round.'

Simple souls, unable to indulge in rhetoric, spoke thus:

Ti Marto: 'The people could perfectly well look at the sun, which appeared to flicker in and out—this way and that. It shot out bundles of light to this side and that and painted everything different colours, the trees and the people, the earth and the air. At a certain moment the sun stopped and then began to dance about till it seemed to be detaching itself from the sky and come on to the heads of the people. It was a terrible moment.'

Lucia's sister Teresa, when Fr. McGlynn asked her if the sun spun round several times and then fell, replied: 'No; it spun round a very short time and as it was spinning it seemed to fall and there was a shower of flowers.' She said they were 'multi-coloured petals', but when they came close enough to be seen what sort they were, they vanished.

Maria Carreira too saw how the sun began to

descend and to move: 'It made different colours—
yellow, blue, white, and shook—shook so much! It
looked like a wheel of fire about to fall on the people.
The people cried out: "Ah, we shall all be killed!"
Others invoked our Lady and made acts of contrition.
At last the sun stopped moving and we all heaved a
sigh of relief: we were still alive and the miracle that
the children had announced had taken place.'

From the opposite cultural extreme I quote, con-
densing it somewhat, from a letter by Dr. A. Garrett,
professor in the University of Coimbra. He says that
he went on looking at the place of the apparitions
(he was standing about 100 yards away on the road
above it). He was calm and cold and his curiosity
was dying down because nothing had happened for a
long time to attract his attention. Then:

'I heard the roar of a thousand voices and saw
that multitude which was spread out at my feet . . .
turn its back to the point on to which up to now it
had been directing all its attention, and look at the
sky on the opposite side. The sun, a few moments
before, had pierced the thick clouds that held it
hidden so that it shone clear and strongly. I turned
towards this magnet which was attracting all eyes and
I could see it like a disc with a clear-cut edge, with
a vivid rim, luminous and shining, but without
hurting one. The comparison that I have heard
made at Fatima with a disc of dull silver, does not
seem to me exact. It was a clearer, more vivid, richer
colour and with shifting tints like the lustre of a
pearl. It was not at all like the moon on a clear
transparent night, for one saw and felt it like a living
star. Nor was it spherical like the moon nor did it
have the same quality of light, nor the moon's shades
of lighter and less light. It looked like a burnished
wheel cut out of mother-o'-pearl. Nor could it be
confused with the sun seen through a fog—there was

no fog.'  (He repeats that it had a clear-cut rim, like a counter used for games.)

He then says that the sky was dappled with light cirrhus clouds with the blue coming through here and there but sometimes you saw it in patches of clear sky: the clouds moved from west to east seeming to pass behind it, or again, taking on tints of pink or diaphanous blue as they passed before it. He was impressed by being able to look at this without pain, save on two occasions when the sun sent out especially bright rays that made one divert one's gaze. This phenomenon lasted about ten minutes.

'This disc span dizzily round. It was not the twinkling of a star: it whirled round upon itself with mad rapidity. Suddenly an outcry was heard like a shriek of anguish uttered by all this multitude. The sun, preserving the celerity of its rotation, detached itself from the firmament and advanced, blood-red, towards the earth, threatening to crush us with the weight of its vast and fiery mass. These moments made a terrifying impression. During this solar phenomenon that I have just described in detail there were changing colours in the air.'

He noticed that everything was becoming darker; he looked further and further off—right on to the horizon—and saw that everything looked amethyst-colour—the things around him, the sky, the air; the shadow of an oak-tree was the same. He began to fear for his eye-sight, turned away, put his hands over his eyes and then turned back—everything still was purple, but not at all like an eclipse; in fact, the atmosphere was clearing.

'Just afterwards, I heard a peasant standing near me exclaim in a voice of amazement: "That lady is yellow!" And, in fact, everything, near and far had changed again and took on the colour of old yellow damask. People looked as if they were suffering from jaundice; I was amused to find them so ugly and repulsive.

'All the phenomena that I have described were observed by me calmly and composedly, without any emotion or being made to jump. It is for others to explain or interpret them.'

It would be tedious to record all the possible descriptions of this event given by eyewitnesses.

The paper *Ordem* said: 'The sun, at one moment surrounded by scarlet flames, at another, aureoled in yellow and deep purple, seemed to be moving very fast and spinning: at times it seemed to be loosed from the sky and to approach the earth, radiating a great heat.'

The contemporary Lisbon paper *O Dia*, October 17, wrote: 'At midday by the sun the rain stopped. The sky, pearly grey in colour, illuminated the vast arid landscape with a strange light. The sun had a transparent gauzy veil so that the eye could easily be fixed on it. The grey mother-o'-pearl tone turned into a sheet of silver which broke up as the clouds were parted and the silver sun, enveloped in the same gauzy grey light, was seen to whirl and turn in the circle of broken clouds. A cry went up from every mouth and people fell on their knees on the muddy ground. . . . The light turned a beautiful blue as though through the window of a cathedral. The blue faded slowly and then the light seemed to pass through yellow glass. Yellow stain fell on white handkerchiefs against the dark skirts of the women. The colours were repeated on the stones and on the Serra.'

Still more significant is what Sr. Avelino de Almeida recorded. For not only was he editor of the secularist paper *O Seculo*, read everywhere, but he had written the day before an article, appearing therefore that very day, quietly derisive of those who proposed to go to Fatima to see a miracle. He, like many other journalists, went to Fatima for the

pleasure of seeing that nothing happened. No advertisement would be more useful for the anti-clericals.
But he was a man of considerable honesty. If his first
article was ironical, his second was no more elusive
than was compatible with truthfulness. He describes
the positively biblical influx of pilgrims; the appalling
weather; the apparition of the sun 'like a silvery
plaque' at which one could look without discomfort:

'It trembles—it makes abrupt movements "outside of all cosmic laws": it dances. It remains for
those competent to pronounce on the macabre
dance of the sun which naturally has impressed—
so witnesses worthy of credence assure me—even
free-thinkers and others not at all interested in
religious matters.' He says that 'most people' saw the
tremulous dance of the sun: others, our Lady; the
colours, the rotation, the 'fall'.

Despite his care to avoid too many direct asser-
tions, the writer was bitterly rebuked by his fellow-
sceptics for having admitted that anything happened
at all.

At the risk of wearying the reader, I will quote
one or two more testimonies, even so reserving others
for a later page.

After a retreat for professional men, Fr. De
Marchi asked a Sr. A. da Silva Santos what his
impressions had been. The day before he had been in
a Lisbon café when a cousin of his entered and said
they were all going to Fatima next day—there were
extraordinary rumours, and they were full of curiosity.
So early on the 13th they went off in three cars.
The first car got lost in the mist, so they arrived at
the Cova only about midday. He was experiencing
no religious emotion. When Lucia called out: 'Look
at the sun!' everyone cried: 'Attention! The sun!' It
left off raining.

'I can hardly find words to describe what followed. The sun began to move and at a certain moment appeared to detach itself from the sky and to be about to hurtle on to us like a wheel of flame. My wife—we had been married only a short time—fainted and I was too upset to look after her; it was my brother-in-law who held her up. I fell on my knees and noticed nothing else and don't know what I said. I think I began to cry like the others.'

Capt. S. C. Osborne sends me the exceptionally interesting witness of Miss N., not a Catholic, who held a position in a Lisbon household: her employers took her, much against her will, to the Cova to see the miracle which was due to happen. She was very sceptical; even during her short stay in Portugal she had heard of visions or miracles in which as 'an ordinary member of the Church of England' she did not believe. They were, she thought, part and parcel of Continental religion, like the worship of saints and images, and she disliked it all. The weather was deplorable; their car broke down; they arrived with tempers badly frayed. They stood on the road looking down into the Cova. But soon the people all began to look up and the rain suddenly stopped—*stopped*, as if cut off by a tap. The heavy clouds did not 'roll away', but through a hole in them you saw the sun. 'It was the colour of stainless steel—like that', she said, pointing to a knife. 'I then saw the sun spin round, and stop, and spin round again.' She cannot remember its 'falling on our heads, as some say', nor whether it 'span' a third time. But it was obvious that the crowds were terrified because they shrieked and cried out for mercy and so forth.

'But I wasn't very impressed by all that for a "miracle". You must remember that I was quite

an ordinary uneducated person and I thought that
perhaps those things happened in Portugal. Nobody
told us that the miracle would have anything to do
with the sun, so I wasn't expecting it. When it came,
I didn't think much of it; but what I have told you
did happen—it is absolutely true.'

Lastly, I mention that the aunt (Portuguese and
Catholic) of a lady whom I have met more than once
in Portugal, and a companion went to Fatima on
October 13th, and knelt with another woman between them. This woman saw all the phenomena,
but the other two saw *nothing at all*. However, as I
shall mention in a moment, the phenomena were seen
and created great disturbance at considerable distances, though they were not thought of in connection
with Fatima.

It seems strange that no attempt was made either
by Catholics or rationalists (so far as I can discover)
to examine this event scientifically. We can anyhow
be sure of two extreme points—*something* happened;
in the face of so much cumulative evidence it would
be impossible to deny that: and again, no one sup-
poses that the sun was physically dislodged from its
place in the solar 'system' or that its gyrations,
approach, and so forth, were material happenings. If
they had been, the solar system (short of many more
miracles) would have been wrecked, or, apart from
that, observatories would have registered some celestial
disturbance. In other words, the witnesses spoke
*secundum apparentias*, according to what it looked like,
as we do when we say 'the sun rises', or, 'the moon
has a halo round it'.

We can also exclude the suggestion of fraud. Who
could have 'faked' the miracle? Not the children.
Not their friends, who did all they could to stop them
going there and were terrified at the prospect. Not

the clergy, who were nearly all hostile to the whole affair; and if we insist on regarding that attitude as a 'smoke-screen' for their real activities, we are still left with the problem of 'how?' *How* could anyone make all that even appear to happen, even in one place, let alone in other places and at considerable distances?

I doubt, too, whether anyone now speaks of 'collective hallucination'. Apart from the extreme improbability of many of the witnesses—sceptic, highly educated, and so forth—succumbing to any hallucination, hallucinations need something to start them off. Thus I knew a group of young men watching for an aeroplane which was to pass over a hill some miles distant. One of them thought he saw it: at once, others thought they did so too. They soon realised their mistake and in fact the aeroplane went another way. But they were *expecting* a plane, and just where they thought they saw it. But the crowds in the Cova were not expecting anything in particular, least of all in the sky, especially as it was raining hard. Even when the sun appeared as a pale disc, that would not have sufficed to make them think it rotated, emitted various colours (to Professor Garrett's eyes the 'yellow' was actually ugly. There was no romanticism about him!) or 'fell' towards the earth. That there was, at first, a general panic, and only afterwards devotion, is assured.

We can then ask if the event could be due to 'natural causes', especially as one investigator tells me that he knows from a trustworthy source that it occurred on other occasions too (*encore parfois*). I asked a Catholic astronomer about this—he was very willing to adduce 'natural causes' if possible. He wrote: 'If we observe a binary star through a moderately large telescope, it is a joy to observe their

gyrations and emissions of different coloured lights—
and this on practically any night in our usually
turbulent atmosphere.' The difficulty about this
would seem to be that the sun is not a binary star
and that no one at the Cova had a telescope large or
small. He made, however, a suggestion that had
occurred also to me, though I am no astronomer. The
air was saturated with moisture; might it not, then,
have acted as a lens, making the sun seem now larger,
now smaller? My friend writes: 'Given layers of air
at different temperatures and densities, I do not see
why they should not produce the same effect as a
series of lenses, and thus account for the observed
result.' My idea was, that the sun, seeming to grow
larger, would inevitably be thought to be approaching
the earth, and from this (especially if it looked
red) the imagination would immediately deduce that
it became hotter and hotter. I recognise that this
hypothesis is very tenuous: but Fr. Rambaud quotes
witnesses (p. 2) who say the sun approached
'doucement', 'peu à peu'.

I also asked myself how the sun, a silvery disc,
could be seen to *rotate* unless it had markings on it.
It is not hinted that it went round in circles about a
central point: Fr. Pio Scatizzi, S.J., however, is quoted
as suggesting that:

'There began to radiate from the centre of the
sun thousands and thousands of monochromatic
lights in sectors, which, in the form of spirals, began
to whirl round the centre of the solar disc in such a
manner that the sun seemed to turn on itself rather
like a Catherine wheel, while the coloured rays spread
out in a centrifugal movement covering the sky as
far as the curtain of clouds, and turning everything
various colours as if by magic. Such a spectacle of
red, yellow, green and violet rays from the sun,

spreading and sweeping over the sky, cannot be explained by any known laws nor has such a thing been seen before.'

Now, first, the writer had said that: 'At midday, suddenly, the heavens opened and the clouds drew back to the horizon leaving the air pure and clear as a mirror.'

But other writers have quite a lot to say about clouds; there seems to me to be a touch of rhetoric here. A little later, he speaks of the sun's 'appearing to fall on the earth in a zigzag path'. But though everyone now writes of this 'zigzag' motion, the first person that I can (so far) find to mention it is Fr. I. L. Pereira, a missionary in India, who, fourteen years later, tells of his experience at school, when he was aged nine and at some ten kilometres from Fatima. An uproar in the street caused the school-mistress to rush out—the children followed her—the sun looked like a 'rotating snowball' and then seemed to fall in a zigzag while the faces of men and things were dyed red, blue, yellow. All thought the world was ending and ran to two chapels.

This testimony is of high importance because it took place far away and no one at first connected it with Fatima any more than the poet Alfonso Lopes Vieira did, who saw it from his verandah forty kilometres off and was 'enchanted' by it (he says nothing about zigzags . . .). On the other hand, it does not allow us to say (with, e.g. the adaptor of Fr. da Fonseca, Canon Barthas, p. 87) that 'all who compose this multitude, all without exception, have the feeling that the sun detaches itself from the sky, and, with zigzag leaps, hurls itself upon them'. It does not matter at all whether the sun appeared to approach in a straight or zigzag line; but we ought not to add up all the details given by various people and offer them as seen by everybody, if only (apart from the impossibility of interrogating 50,000-70,000 people) because everybody did *not* see the same thing, and at least two (as I have said) saw nothing at all.

We have to discard, then, all suggestion that the sky was perfectly clear. Fr. McGlynn quotes from a letter (p. 177) which says that the clouds rushed dizzily to the sides so that the sky around the sun 'was completely clear of clouds'. 'All this (i.e. the various phenomena) passed "in a few seconds".' But he also quotes (pp. 177-183) a long account given by Senhor Mendes (alluded to above, p. 44). Some charcoal burners had told him of the apparitions at Torres Novas, and he and a friend rode to Aljustrel, and he was so impressed by the candour of the children that he went with them to the Cova, where he said the rosary with them, and could pray without any distraction. He then wrote to his fiancée saying how impressed he had been. He returned for September 13: people said they saw rays and a shining shower, but he saw nothing. He is a very large man and picked Lucia up to speak to the people; but she struggled so hard and kept saying so petulantly 'leave me alone' that he lost all faith in her and the apparitions. Reluctantly he drove his brother and others to the Cova on October 13, but said he would stay in the car. Yet he found himself, without knowing how, close to the children. He says (this does not seem accurate) that Lucia called out: 'Look at the sun. The Lady is going to manifest herself.' Then he says (and also wrote): 'The rain stopped: the clouds split up into tatters—thin, transparent strips. The sun was seen as a crown of fire, empty in the middle. It turned round on itself and moved across the sky. It could be seen behind the clouds and in between them rolling around

and moving horizontally. The crowd prayed in terror,'
and, says he, his own hair stood on end. He did not
see the colours or other phenomena, nor could he
tell how long the apparition lasted. This time, too,
he lifted Lucia up and put her on a rock: she made
no resistance but spoke to the people 'as if she were
preaching'—'Do penance! Our Lady wants you to do
penance!' Senhor Mendes is alone in saying that the
sun looked like a ring: the version given by the
editor of *O Seculo* corresponds more nearly with that
given by the children and most of the onlookers. It is
interesting to observe how people saw (or remembered) what was substantially the same thing in so
many different ways.

It will be remembered that the Jews wanted our
Lord to give them a 'sign in the sky' and that He
refused it. 'Coercive' miracles are not to be expected.
Perhaps even Lucia wanted more than she should,
when she asked for a miracle such that all would *have*
to believe. St. Thomas says that it may be hard,
at times, to distinguish a miracle from a 'portent':
one has to see the event in its setting: our Lord's own
miracles were not isolated events nor ends in themselves, but woven into His whole Messianic career,
and 'signs' meant to lead witnesses to something
further still. In this case, the whole episode of 'Fatima'
seems to me manifestly spiritual: the children had
asserted that a great marvel would be worked at just
that time and place; no one knew what sort of marvel
to expect: the event that did take place was such as
at first to throw a vast multitude into panic. Yet not
all saw precisely the same thing, as Lucia herself
was to acknowledge: I presume that each received
what he or she was prepared for or what God knew to
be needed, as maybe, when the divine Voice spoke
to our Lord, some said: An Angel spoke to Him;

others that it thundered (John xii. 29). So far as I know, I have been strictly true to the evidence in what I have written; and I can find no rationalist explanation of the events taken as a whole which seems in the least adequate. It is true that those events may seem to us strange rather than devotional; but I am not sure that we do not start slightly prejudiced by the popular and also journalistic expression—'the sun *danced*'. Further, it is rightly said that such a phenomenon may seem very different to one who sees it from what it does to one who merely reads about it: and finally, it is not for us to judge what best suits the imagination of a multitude chiefly composed of Portuguese peasantry: I don't know what sort of miracle would most appeal to the sophisticated English mentality.[1]

[1] The following interesting passage has kindly been sent to me by Fr. V. Turner, S.J., from a letter of the Bishop of Magona in Minorca (A.D. 418? Migne, *P.L.*, 20, 472). 'At about 7 o'clock we began solemnly to celebrate the Sunday Mass, for while we were instructing—or cataloguing (for we wrote down their names)—the Jews who were coming to the faith of Christ, the greater part of the day had passed by. The church is built a little way off from the town and in a lonely place, and in it the relics of the holy martyr Stephen have recently been put and there repose, and here we and all the people were awaiting Mass. Now two monks, whom God had forechosen to be witnesses of His marvels, were lying on the grass of the field which spread in front of the church doors. A worthy citizen called Julius with another man was on his way to the church and was just beginning to pass by them when one of the monks, looking up, saw a wonderful sight and in his bewilderment uttered a wild shout, and then, recovering himself, pointed his hand at what he had seen, and could not express it in words. There was a sort of mass of brilliant light, about the size of a man, and like the vessels commonly called 'orcas' ('oreas'?), but so dazzling bright that it seemed to the Brother who saw it first (and we know this from his own lips) as though the sun were falling down. This, so it seemed to them, slid slowly across the basilica in which we and all the people were sitting. Yet it seemed so close that this same Brother, terrorstruck, began to run away thinking it had fallen behind the basilica; but he stopped, since the other Brother pulled him back. For he had seen the same thing but it had been further off, at least, said he, he

## III

Lucia had said there would be other visions on that day. Canon Formigão, with sound critical sense, decided he must visit them that very evening, lest fatigue should dull their memories or suggestions distort them or lest they might be accused of having had time in which to concoct a unanimous story. He evicted importunate visitors and began with Lucia. I cannot but feel that the following interrogations seem not only unusually repetitive but to keep less closely to the point, which was that day's apparition. This may be due to the excitement of the hour or to fatigue.

'Did our Lady appear again today?'
'Yes.'
'Was she dressed as before?'
'In the same way.'
'Did St. Joseph and the Holy Child appear?'
'Yes.'
'Did anyone else appear?'
'Our Lord appeared and blessed the people and our Lady of the two cards.'
'What do you mean, our Lady of the two cards?'
'Our Lady appeared dressed like Our Lady of Sorrows but without the sword in her heart, and our Lady dressed I don't know how but I think it was Our Lady of Carmel.'
'They all came at the same time, didn't they?'
(The Canon writes that he was rather nervous about this leading question: 'though it would not have been strictly impossible for the children to have had a simultaneous vision of the three forms of the Blessed Virgin, it would clearly have created a

thought so but was not sure. Further, certain women, Jewesses, looking out of the dining-room, saw it too, and they too thought it had fallen over (behind) the basilica. Now whether this apparition was an angel or Stephen himself, is uncertain.'

serious difficulty.' That is, normal consciousness requires to assimilate one fact after another, which takes time; but a direct preternatural 'vision', however complex, can be timeless.)

'No; first I saw Our Lady of the Rosary, then St. Joseph and the Holy Child. Then I saw our Lord, then Our Lady of Sorrows and at the end what I think was Our Lady of Carmel.'

'Was the Child standing or was He being carried by St. Joseph?'

'He was being carried.'

'Was He already big?'

'He was little.'

'How old could He be?'

'About one year.'

'Why did you say that at one moment the Lady seemed to you dressed like Our Lady of Carmel?'

'Because she had things hanging from her hand.'

'Did they appear on the top of the *carrasqueira?*'

'No; near the sun, after the Lady had disappeared from the tree.'

'Was our Lord standing?'

'I saw Him only from the waist up.'

'How long did the apparition on the *carrasqueira* last? Enough to say a rosary?'

'Not so long, I think.'

'Did the figures you saw in the sun last long?'

'A short time.'

'Did the Lady say who she was?'

'She said she was the Lady of the Rosary.'

'Did you ask her what she wanted?'

'Yes—she said we must amend ourselves and not offend our Lord who was too much offended and must say the rosary and beg pardon for our sins.'

'Did she say anything else?'

'She said a chapel must be built at the Cova da Iria.'

'How was money for building it to be got?'

'I suppose it would be what was left there.'

'Did she say anything about our soldiers killed in the war?'

'No, she said nothing.'

'Did she tell you to tell the people to look at the sun?'

'No.'

'Did she say the people were to do penance?'

'Yes.'

'Did she use the word penance?'

'No. She said we were to say the rosary and amend our sins and beg pardon of our Lord, but she did not use the word penance.'

'When did the sign in the sun begin? After the Lady disappeared?'

'Yes.'

'Did you see the Lady come?'

'Yes; from the east.'

'And the other times?'

'I didn't look the other times.'

'Did you see her go?'

'Yes, towards the east.'

'How did she disappear?'

'Little by little.'

'What disappeared first?'

'Her head. Then her body, and the last thing that I saw was her feet.'

'Did she go with her back away from or towards the people?'

'With her back towards them.'

'Did she take long to disappear?'

'Only a short time.'

'Was she surrounded with any light?'

'I saw her in the middle of a splendour. This time too she blinded me. Sometimes I had to rub my eyes.'

'Will our Lady come back to appear?'

'I don't think she will. She said nothing about it.'

'Will you return to the Cova on the 13th?'

'No.'

'Will the Lady work any miracles? cure any sick
persons?'

'I don't know. I told her today I had various
petitions and she said she would grant some and not
others . . . she did not say when she would grant
them.'

'What is the title of the chapel in the Cova to be?'

'She said today that she was the Lady of the
Rosary.'

'Did she say that many people are to go there
from all parts?'

'She didn't say anyone was to go there.'

'Did you see the signs in the sun?'

'I saw it going round.'

'Did you see signs on the tree?'

'No.'

'When was the Lady more beautiful, this time or
the others?'

'The same.'

'How long was her dress?'

'It went down below the middle of her legs.'

'What colour was our Lady when she was near
the sun?'

'The mantle was blue and the dress white.'

'And our Lord, and St. Joseph, and the Child?'

'St. Joseph was bright red (*encarnado*)[1] and I think
our Lord and the Child were too.'

'When did you ask the Lady to make the people
believe in her apparition?'

'I asked her several times. The first time I asked
her was in June, I think.'

'When did she tell you the secret?'

'I think it was the second time.' (See p. 40.)

The Canon went on to Jacinta: 'Besides our Lady,
whom did you see today in the Cova?'

'St. Joseph and the Holy Child.'

---

[1] I think it is only by a slip that Fr. De Marchi (p. 166, copied
by Walsh) says St. Joseph was in white.

'Where did you see them?'

'Near the sun.'

'What did the Lady say?'

'That we were to say the rosary every day and that the war would end today.'

'To whom did she say that?'

'To Lucia and to me. Francisco didn't hear.'

'Did you hear her say when the soldiers would come back?'

'No.'

'What else did she say?'

'That a chapel was to be built in the Cova da Iria.'

'Where did she come from?'

'From the east . . . and she went back to the east.'

'Did she go backwards facing the people?'

'No; she turned her back to the people.'

'Did she say she would come back to the Cova?'

'She said before that that it was the last time she would come, and today, too, she said it was the last time.'

'Did she say anything else?'

'That we were to say the rosary every day to Our Lady of the Rosary.'

'Where did she say people were to say it?'

'She didn't say where.'

'Did she say they were to go to the church?'

'No; she never said that.'

'Where do you like saying the rosary best, here at home, or in the Cova?'

'In the Cova.'

'Why?'

'I don't know' (*por nada*).

'With what money did she say the chapel was to be built?'

'She said a chapel was to be built. I don't know about the money.'

'Did you look at the sun? Did you see the signs?'

'Yes.'

'Did the Lady tell you to look at the sun?'

'No.'

'Then how did you see the signs?'

'I turned my head to that side.'

'Was the Child Jesus to the right or the left of St. Joseph?'

'To the right.'

'Was He standing or being carried?'

'He was standing.'

'Did you see St. Joseph's right arm?'

'No.'

'How tall was the Child? Did He come up to St. Joseph's chest?'

'He didn't reach his waist.'

'How old do you think He was?'

'He was like Deolinda das Neves' (a child of about two).

Next, Francisco.

'Did you see our Lady this time?'

'Yes.'

'What Lady was she?'

'The Lady of the Rosary.'

'How was she dressed?'

'In white, with a rosary in her hand.'

'Did you see St. Joseph and the Child?'

'Yes—beside the sun.'

'Was the Child being carried by St. Joseph or at his side? was He big or little?'

'Little.'

'Was He the size of Deolinda das Neves?'

'Just that size.'

'How did the Lady hold her hands?'

'Joined.'

'Did you see her on the *carrasqueira* or by the sun as well?'

'By the sun as well.'

'Which was brighter or more shining, the sun or the Lady's face?'

'The Lady's face was brighter. The Lady was white.'

'Did you hear what the Lady said?'

'I heard nothing of what she said.'

'Who told you the secret? the Lady?'

'No. Lucia told me.'

'Can you tell it?'

'I'm not telling it.'

'You won't tell it because you're afraid of being beaten by Lucia. Isn't that so?'

'No.'

'Then why don't you tell it? Is it a sin to tell it?'

'Perhaps it is a sin to tell it.'

'Is the secret for the good of your soul and Lucia's and Jacinta's?'

'Yes.'

'For the good of Fr. Ferreira's soul?'

'I don't know.'

'Would the people be sad if they knew it?'

'Yes.'

'From which side did the Lady come?'

'From the east—and she went back to the east.'

'Did she go backwards?'

'She turned her back to us.'

'Slowly or quickly?'

'Slowly.'

'Did she walk as we do?'

'She didn't walk. She just went, without moving her feet.'

'What part of the Lady disappeared first?'

'Her head.'

'Did you see her well, like the other times?'

'I saw her better than last month.'

'Was she most beautiful now, or the other times?'

'As beautiful now as last month.'

Jacinta's statement that the Lady had said that the war was ending that day naturally upset the Canon and he returned to Aljustrel on October 19 in the afternoon. He found the children in Ti Marto's house being examined by a Fr. Lacerda, a chaplain in the Portuguese Expeditionary Force on leave, and wishing to see the children before he returned to France. There was also another priest, from Leiria, and the Fatima parish-priest. The children were utterly exhausted by all they had been through, and Lucia especially seemed unable to recall details that she remembered before, and she found it difficult to attend. The Canon, however, was both kindly and persistent, and apparently went straight to the point.

'Did our Lady say, on October 13, that the war was ending that same day? What words did she use?'

'She said thus: "The war is finishing today. You may expect your soldiers very soon."' [1]

'But you see that the war is still going on. The papers say that there has been fighting since the 13th. How do you explain that, if our Lady said the war was finishing that day?'

'I don't know. I only know that I heard her say that the war was finishing on the 13th: I don't know anything more.'

'Some people say that they heard you say on that day that our Lady declared that the war was finishing soon. Is that true?'

'I said exactly what our Lady said.'

'On the 27th of last month I came to your house to talk with you. Do you remember?'

'I remember seeing you here.'

'Well, on that day you said that our Lady said that she would come with St. Joseph and the Child Jesus and that afterwards the war would end—not on that day.'

[1] The next question concerns only the exact turn of Portuguese phrasing used. *Ela disse 'esperem cá pelos seus militares' ou 'esperai cá vossos soldados'?* The former, which Lucia said was used, is slightly less conventional than the latter.

'I can't remember now just how she said it. She may have said that; I don't know. Perhaps I didn't understand the Lady properly.'

'On the 13th, do you remember telling the people to look at the sun?'

'I don't remember doing that.'

'Did you tell them to shut their umbrellas?'

'The other months I did; I don't remember about this last time.'

'Did you know when the sign in the sun was going to begin?'

'No—I looked; it looked like the moon.'

'Why did you look at the sun?'

'I looked, because all the people said I should look at it.'

'Did our Lady say that she would pray to her divine Son for the souls of the soldiers who had died in the war?'

'No, Father.'

'Did she say that the people would be punished if they did not amend their sins?'

'I can't remember if she said that: I think not.'

'On the 13th you didn't have any doubts about what the Lady said. How do you account for the doubts you have now?'

'I remembered better then. It was not so long ago.'

The Canon turned for a moment to a different subject.

'What did you see about a year ago? Your mother said that you and some other children had seen a form (*vulto*) wrapped in a cloth so that you couldn't see its face. Why did you tell me last month that it was nothing? [This shows that the Canon had had at least one un-recorded conversation.]

(No answer.)

'Did you run away that time?'

'I think I ran away.' (See pp. 144, 150.)

'On the 11th of this month you did not want to
tell me that our Lord would appear blessing the people
and Our Lady of Sorrows. Was that because you
thought I would laugh at you as other people did
and say it was impossible? Or was it because there
were so many other strangers there and you did not
want to say it in front of them?'

(No answer.)

'When did our Lady tell you there would be
those other apparitions on October 13?'

'The day she appeared to me at Valinhos or
another 13th. I don't know for sure.'

'Did you see our Lord?

'I saw a figure that appeared to be a man; it
seemed to be our Lord.'

'Where was this figure?'

'Beside the sun.'

'Did you see it blessing the people?'

'No; but our Lady said our Lord would come to
bless the people.'

'If the people knew the secret that our Lady told
you, would they be sad?'

'I think they would be as they are—about the
same.'

The Canon now interrogated Francisco.

'Did you see our Lord bless the people on the
13th of this month?'

'No. I saw only our Lady.'

'Did you see Our Lady of Carmel and of Sorrows?'

'No. Our Lady seemed the one I saw before. She
was dressed in the same way.'

'Did you look at the sun?'

'Yes.'

'Did you see St. Joseph and the Child Jesus?'

'Yes.'

'Were they near or far from the sun?'

'Near.'

'Which side was St. Joseph?'

'On the left.'

'And our Lady?'

'On the right.'

'Where was the Child Jesus?'

'Beside St. Joseph.'

'Which side?'

'I didn't notice which side.'

'Was the child big or small?'

'Small.'

'When our Lady was over the tree, did you hear what she said to Lucia? did you see her laugh?'

(No, to all this: it seemed as if she were not speaking. Then come the questions about the sun, quoted above.)

The Canon then questioned Jacinta, walking with her along the road.

'On the 13th of this month did you see our Lord near the sun and Our Lady of Sorrows and of Carmel?'

'No.'

'But on the 11th, you said they would appear.'

'I did. It was Lucia who saw the other Lady. I did not.'

'Did you see St. Joseph?'

'I did. Lucia said St. Joseph was giving the peace.'

(The questions about the sun follow.)

'What did the Lady say this last time?'

'She said: "I have come here to tell you that people must not offend our Lord any more because He is very much offended, and that if people amend their lives the war will end, and if they do not the world will end." Lucia heard better than I what the Lady said.'

'Did she say that the war would end that day, or shortly?'

'Our Lady said that the war would end when she went to heaven.'

'But the war has not ended!'

'It is ending! It is ending!'

'But when will it end?'
'I think it will end on Sunday.'

It may be worth while to interpolate a brief comment on this. On July 8, 1924, Lucia said: 'I think our Lady added this—"People must be converted. The war will end today and the soldiers can be expected soon." However my cousin Jacinta told me afterwards at home that our Lady had said: "People must be converted. The war will end within a year." I was so preoccupied with all the petitions they had wanted me to put before our Lady that I did not give all my attention to her words.' I am much more surprised by the last sentence than by the children getting confused about dates—'time' does not mean very much to children; and they *do* want everything to happen 'today'!—but how could Lucia have attended to anything save what our Lady was actually saying to her? Anyhow, I do not think that *O Seculo* or any other contemporary document reports that the children had said 'today'. If they had said 'today' surely every anti-clerical paper would at once have made capital out of so substantial a mistake? No definitive solution is possible: but we may conclude that our Lady connected the war with sin, and its termination with conversion; and we may even surmise that if the after-war is quite as distressing as the war itself, that is because men have *not* been converted.

Canon Formigão went back to interrogate the children again on November 2. He began with Jacinta, but her replies are almost entirely repetitions of what has already been written. She added that the Lady's feet were white and that she thought she wore stockings, that she thought the secret was revealed in July; in June, after telling Lucia that she must learn to read and saying that she would cure and convert some but not others, the Lady said nothing else. At the Valinhos Lucia asked if she might bring her Manuel (was this her father and was it to the Cova that she asked if she might bring him?) and the Lady said she could bring everybody. 'She said that if they had not taken us to Ourém St. Joseph would come with the Child to give peace to the world: and Our Lady of the Rosary with two angels, one on each side.' She repeated that on October 13 the Lady had said that the war ended that day. 'She said that the people must make a chapel and I don't know if she said "for the Lady of the Rosary or that she was the Lady of the Rosary".'

The Canon then asked Lucia:
'Did the Lady wear stockings? are you sure of that?'
'I think they were stockings but perhaps they weren't.'
'You once said that the Lady wore stockings. Were they stockings or were they feet?'
'If they were stockings they were white; but I don't know for sure if they were stockings or her feet.'
'Was the dress always the same length?'
'The last time it seemed longer.'
'You have never told the secret nor even said that the people would be sad if they knew it. Francisco and Jacinta said they would be sad. If you cannot say this neither can they say it. What do you think?'
'I don't know whether or not they should say that the people would be sad. Our Lady said we were not to say anything to anyone. So I can't say anything.'
As for Francisco he added nothing new, save that the Lady near the sun looked the same as the one he saw below; and No, he had not seen our Lord.

This brings us to the end of the contemporary history of the Apparitions and of the examination of the children. It is evident that there are a few gaps in the records, for example, the Canon, we saw, must have had an interview with Maria Rosa about the 'sheeted form': we hear only on November 2 from Jacinta about a promised apparition of our Lady between two angels, and we are not told whether the *andores* were made and carried in procession. Still, when we remember how splintered and scattered is the evidence out of which we construct Roman or Greek 'history', I am not at all troubled by such insignificant gaps. The narrative, taken as a whole, seems to me 'all of a piece' and as realistic as possible, especially when we recall the extremely personal evidence given by Ti Marto and Maria Carreira. I cannot detect the intrusion of any alien or 'literary' element, anything 'decorative' merely—in short, of any expression that would not quite naturally have been used by the various persons concerned.[1]

As for the discrepancies in the children's accounts (of which presumably the more important are the dating of the end of the war and whether the Holy Child was standing by St. Joseph or was carried by him), one must recall that they were very small, totally unused to anything outside their peasant-circle, and suddenly thrust into an astonishing notoriety, heckled and harried even by the clergy

[1] I think it just possible that the story of La Salette and of Lourdes may have sunk deeper into Lucia's memory than she guessed, if only because of the use of the word 'chapel' which, since Lourdes, has become almost traditional in such narratives. Our Lady can hardly have asked for a 'chapel' if what she really wanted was only a chapel, and not a large basilica; on the other hand, such children may well have thought of the parish church alone as a church—in lonely districts any other sanctuary probably was a small shrine or chapel, and the children could hardly imagine or foresee anything grander.

with whom for the first time in their lives they had to disagree, driven half off their heads by alternate flattery and mockery, to say nothing of the physical ill-treatment that Lucia at any rate had to endure within her home: in spite of all this they were—even Jacinta!—firm as a rock about the 'secret'. Again (we shall have to return to this below) whatever was 'given' to them was given in the way most suited to each. Thus Francisco never heard anything; neither he nor Jacinta saw all the visions 'near the sun' and Jacinta heard less clearly than Lucia did: Lucia heard, but only (she was to say) so as to be able to give the 'sense' of what our Lady said: even she could be distracted by her own thoughts, and (as we shall also see) her memory was not perfect. The only element that strikes me as strange is that St. Joseph (and, they 'thought', the Holy Child) was dressed in scarlet, a colour in which he is not, so far as I know, represented in Portugal or anywhere else. I suppose the children saw him and the Child in the way that most appealed to each. This holds good throughout: many thousands were thrown into wonderment and even panic by the 'miracle of the sun', yet not all saw that or other phenomena in the same way, or at all.

There was another phenomenon that needs to be mentioned because it was recurrent and could be photographed. This was the appearance of a shower of white objects (Lucia's sister Teresa said: 'multi-coloured') which some called snow-flakes, or rose-petals, or white globules which fell from the direction of the sun, being larger the higher up they were, and vanishing when it seemed that the hand might actually catch them. This was seen on September 12, 1917; and on May 13 in 1918 and in 1924. On the last occasion Antonio Rebélo Martins, Portuguese vice-consul in the U.S.A., was present and photographed the phenomenon. On the verso of the print are the signatures of various witnesses, the whole being officially attested and stamped by a notary. To my eye, the print shows a sort of white cascade starting from a point in the top left-hand corner and fanning out till it becomes diaphanous towards the foot of the print. It also contains brighter, divergent streaks, and these are crossed by three, perhaps four, fainter horizontal streaks behind the diagonal ones. Of course a moving substance would create the impression of a 'streak' upon the plate, just as a star, if the exposure lasted long enough, would seem like a smudge, not a point. Looking carefully towards the left of the lower part of this photograph I can discern several small white dots with a very short dark line beneath them, in which some writers profess to discern a 'shadow'. I have not met anyone who can explain this to me, and certainly I cannot explain it myself, nor can I see any religious significance in it. Possibly, if it was preternatural, it served to arouse the attention of onlookers to something that should be still more wonderful because more spiritual, and we might recall how our Lord *began* with 'startling' Nathanael by showing He had seen him under the fig tree, and the woman of Samaria by reading her conscience. We cannot dictate what 'signs and marvels' God shall show to men; and it is evident that not all such signs would be equally impressive to everyone.

CHAPTER 6

## AGITATED INTERSPACE

THESE events in no way modified the blind
fanaticism of that anti-clerical period. The
Masonic Lodge of Santarém, together with men from
Vila Nova de Ourém, went to the Cova during the
night of October 23-24. They cut down the *azinheira*
tree (only they chose the wrong one: the real one was
by now a mere stump) and removed the wooden
arch, the lanterns, the two crosses and the little altar-
table. All this was put on exhibition near the Santarém
seminary. You had to pay to enter it: the profits were
to be given to a local charity—the Misericordia. The
director, however, refused to accept it. A procession
was formed in which the various exhibits were carried
to the sound of 'blasphemous litanies' and the beating
of two drums. The police finally dispersed it. The
*Seculo* itself denounced the whole business as a disgrace—Catholics were forbidden to hold processions
though they formed practically the whole population
and though their ceremonies involved no attack on
the convictions of others. Protests came pouring in.
Perhaps no anti-clerical action could have been more
calculated to arouse every sentiment of decency in a
land which still had to endure régimes so chaotic
and so savage that by now they seem to outstrip the
limits of caricature itself.

This did not, however, check the attack on the
children and their story. A certain José Vale, editor
of *O Mundo*, a hard drinker and a violent atheist and
something of an anarchist, flooded the district with
scurrilous pamphlets invoking all liberal-minded
persons to assemble at the Fatima church .and

unmask the 'comedy'. The parish-priest, alarmed,
transferred the Sunday Mass to a chapel of Our Lady
of Ortiga, some distance off. The children and others
of their family were taken to a *quinta* six kilometres
distant where a young man, Pedro Caupers, of
reliable disposition, was staying. Ti Marto relates the
adventure—for such it was for these poor peasants,
flying, says he, like the Holy Family from persecution.
Happily his sense of caustic humour never deserted
him and he remembered every detail.

They started an hour after sunrise and reached
the chapel of the house only to find it packed and
that Mass had reached the offertory. But a servant
escorted them to the family-tribune so that they heard
Mass from above the altar. Don Pedro came up and
asked Lucia to say the rosary just where she was. She
was shy, but ended by saying it. Don Pedro remarked
that she always said one Hail Mary too many. Ti
Marto said: 'But, Don Pedro, that Hail Mary belongs
to the Our Father and that makes eleven. I always do
that when I pray alone. I've always been taught that
the *Pater* isn't complete without an *Ave*.' They then had
some food and a servant showed them over the house.
'Such huge rooms! Every time Lucia went into one,
she exclaimed: "Oh what a barrack!" The servants
kept saying: "Lucia, do you want to see another
barrack?" ' In the end, they saw the whole house.
Then Don Pedro sent for three lambs and photographed the children with the lambs on their shoulders.
Then they had some more to eat and then Pedro
asked Ti Marto if he would stay with Francisco since
he himself had to go to Vargos and had room in his
car only for the two little girls. So Ti Marto and
Francisco went for a long walk all round the property.
The car returned late; and it was dark when they all
of them came home to Aljustrel.

Meanwhile at Fatima an unintended 'comedy' had been played out. The rioters arrived but found no one there save one official. Not knowing what to do, they went off to the Cova. But alas, men from two neighbouring villages had collected a number of donkeys, and by rubbing something on their noses made them all bray. Moreover, round the stump of the *azinheira* had been put a lot of fodder proper to such beasts. 'We did it', says Maria Carreira, 'to annoy them.' They certainly succeeded. Some hid; others climbed into trees; when an invader said anything specially offensive they all shouted, 'Blessed be Jesus and Mary'. Then the men and boys who had been to Mass at Ortiga arrived and started to call out at the orators: 'Donkeys! beasts!' only to be answered by cries of 'Country oafs and fools!' In the end they all went away and nothing was seen of them again.[1]

[1] The following extracts from a freemason pamphlet may illustrate the sort of thing that was being circulated. 'To all liberal Portuguese! Reaction gallops ahead! The Association for Civil Registration and the Portuguese Federation of Freethinkers energetically protest against the ridiculous comedy of Fatima—Citizens! . . . As if the pernicious propaganda of reactionaries were not enough, we now see a *miracle* produced in order further to degrade the people into fanaticism and superstition. There has been staged . . . a disgraceful comedy at Fatima at which thousands of people have assisted, a ridiculous spectacle in which the simple folk have been ingeniously deceived by means of collective suggestion into a belief in a supposed apparition of the mother of Jesus of Nazareth to three children tricked into this shameful spectacle for the commercial purposes of clerical reaction!—As if however the declarations of these poor little dupes who affirm that they have seen a 'Virgin' (whom, however, nobody else can see or hear) were not enough, it is affirmed, or rather invented, that the sun, at a certain hour on October 13, 1917 (the eighth anniversary of the assassination of Francisco Ferrer) and in the height of the twentieth century, was seen to dance a fandango in the clouds! . . . This, citizens, is a miserable and retrograde attempt to plunge the Portuguese people once more into the dense darkness of past times which have departed never to return. The Republic, whose citizens are charged with the noble and ungrateful task of guiding it into the glorious paths of Civilisation and Progress, cannot consent to the degradation of the people into fanaticism and credulity, for this

The spate of anti-clerical propaganda, whether fierce or fatuous, still failed to act as a deterrent; in fact, more and more people came to the Cova and left money there. Since no chapel was being built, it began to be rumoured that Maria Carreira and her husband were using the money for their own purposes. The Cardinal Patriarch wrote to the local priest that the money should be kept by some reliable person but not by the children's parents. Santos, the Administrator, sent for Sr. Carreira, who denied all knowledge of who kept the money. Maria rather startlingly assured other enquirers that she had hidden the money in a tin under a stone and it had been stolen. It would seem that at first everyone heard and believed this and then that nobody did. Finally Maria went to the parish-priest and asked if they might not begin to build the chapel. He did not refuse permission, but would not take any part in the matter. Abóbora was very annoyed not only because nothing would grow in the Cova any more, but because people

would be an unpardonable failure in their primal duty not only towards their country but to Humanity as a whole. It is therefore our duty to demand from the public authorities the most energetic and immediate precautions against this shameless plan by which reaction seeks to plunge the people once more into medievalism. . . . What shall be our means of co-operation with those from whom we claim the action necessary for the end which we envisage? An intensive and tenacious propaganda which will raise the mentality of our co-citizens to the realms of Truth, Reason, and Science, convincing them that nothing can alter the laws of Nature and that the pretended miracles are nothing but miserable tricks to abuse the credulity which is the child of ignorance. . . . Let professors in schools and colleges educate their children in a rational manner, liberating them from religious preconceptions as from all others. . . . Let us then liberate ourselves and cleanse our minds not only from foolish beliefs in such gross and laughable tricks as Fatima, but more especially in any credence in the supernatural and in an alleged God omnipotent, omniscient and omni-everything, instrument of the subtle imagination of rogues who want to capture popular credulity for their purposes.—Citizens! Long live the Republic! Down with Reaction! Long live Liberty!

began cutting down not only twigs, but whole
branches of trees there. However, he gave in, and
said they could make a chapel as big as they liked.
Endless difficulties arose because everyone had different ideas about it, and no priest would interfere
with the planning. At last the stone-mason, a devout
man, said that if it was God's work there was bound
to be trouble about it at first, so they persevered, and
within a month a small and very simple chapel was
built, but for a long time no statue was placed within
it.

While these events were proceeding the children
had to live their lives as best they could. Happily
they met at last a sympathetic priest, Fr. Faustino
Ferreira of Olival, who won their entire confidence
and encouraged them never to reveal the secret, even
to the clergy who were always trying to make them
tell it. It was he who instructed them in the matter
of 'making sacrifices'.

'If you specially want to eat something, eat something else and offer the sacrifice to God. If you want
to play, offer that too. If you are obliged to answer
questions, that then is God's will and you can offer
Him one more sacrifice.'

Now if the children had, much earlier, embarked
on their career of habitual and heroic penance it may
seem strange that this sort of very simple recom-
mendation was needed. My surmise—it can be no
more than that—is that the children certainly had
got the idea of making sacrifices for sinners well into
their heads, and very likely had begun a whole
series of experimental penances, some of them unwise,
such as eating bitter acorns instead of their lunch,
passing the whole day without drinking, and so forth.
Experience has made it well known to what lengths
even quite young children may go in the direction of

'mortification'. I think it possible that Fr. Faustino
was a guide rather than a stimulus, and led them
away from exterior imprudences to a deeper kind of
sacrifice, that of their own will. Lucia was to bear
witness to the increasing 'seriousness' of Jacinta, to
whom—according to the official testimony of the
parish-priest—our Lady appeared at least three
times between October 1917 and August 1918. It
must have been during this time that she made her
first Communion, and the evidence seems to me
continuous that she became increasingly sensitive to
the horror of sin and to the duty of offering every
possible sacrifice to save souls from falling into hell.
As for Francisco, two ladies came one day and asked
him what he would like to be—a carpenter? a soldier?
a doctor? a priest, surely, so that he could say Mass
and preach? To all this he answered No, adding that
he didn't want to be anything but to die and go to
heaven. Ti Marto was present and vouches for this,
and regarded it as another 'great proof'.

Though the following incidents, proper to this
time, were written down by Lucia much later, yet
most of them seem to me entirely 'in tune with' the
last part of Francisco's brief life for all of which
Ti Marto is a reliable eyewitness. Thus, one day the
children were pasturing their flocks and had separated
the better to keep an eye on them. Francisco had been
away a long time and Lucia felt anxious. She sent
Jacinta to look for him and the child called him
several times but without result. Lucia finally found
him prostrate behind a wall. She shook him by the
shoulder and asked him what he was doing. As
though waking from a deep sleep he said he had begun
to say the Angel's prayer (see p. 145) and had then
started to 'think'.

'Didn't you hear Jacinta call?'

'No; I didn't hear anything.'

Another time he went off by himself, and after a while Jacinta found him praying behind a rock. She told him to come and have lunch. He said he didn't want any: they could call him when they said the rosary.

Then Lucia said: 'What were you doing all that time?'

'I was thinking of God who is so sad because of all the sins. If only I could comfort Him!'

This notion of 'consoling God' did indeed dominate the boy. Lucia also says that he observed:

'I loved seeing the angel and I loved seeing our Lady even more, but what I liked best of all was seeing our Lord in that light which God put into our hearts. I love God so much, but He is so sad because of all the sins. We mustn't commit even the tiniest sin.'

It is well remarked that his wish for heaven was not so much for his own sake as for the 'consolation of God' to which he could there entirely devote himself.

'Soon Jesus will come and take me to heaven with Him and then I shall always be able to comfort Him.'

It is not surprising that the prayers of the children were so valued that they were asked even for miracles. Most of these stories are rather vague and cannot now be examined into; but I relate one because it has a flavour of its own, and is, I feel, somehow characteristic of the people and the place.

Lucia had an aunt Vitoria who lived in Fatima. She had a son who was considered a wastrel and some time previously had disappeared from Fatima. Vitoria came to ask Lucia's prayers for him; but not finding her she asked Jacinta to pray. The child did

so; and after a few days the young man came home
and asked for forgiveness. He then went to Aljustrel
to say what happened. He had stolen some money,
had spent it, had been arrested and imprisoned in
Torres Novas. He had escaped and had hidden in
some pine-woods in the hills. Night fell; he thought
he was hopelessly lost; frightened by the dark and
the wind, he knelt and prayed. After a little, he saw
Jacinta, who took him by the hand and put him on
a road along which she signed to him to walk. At
daybreak he found himself near a village he knew
and went straight home, overwhelmed with emotion.
Lucia asked Jacinta if indeed she had been there;
she said she did not so much as know those hills or
woods, but that she had felt so sorry for their aunt
Vitoria that she had prayed very hard for the young
man.

## CHAPTER 7

# THE RECALL OF FRANCISCO AND JACINTA

IN October 1918 the whole Marto family save Ti
Marto himself went down with Spanish influenza.[1]

Ti Marto had to do not only all his own work,
but all the nursing, and felt that God indeed was
helping him, since he never had to beg for anything.
There were improvements and relapses, but Jacinta
and Francisco were sure that they would soon die,
and Jacinta, one day, told Lucia that our Lady had
come and said that she would fetch Francisco very
soon. Lucia added that our Lady had asked Jacinta
if she would like to convert some more sinners; that
she had answered Yes; and that our Lady had then
said that she would go to two hospitals, that her
mother, but not Lucia, would take her there, and
that then she would be alone.

It is Olimpia who tells us how docile Francisco
was during his illness: he would never express preferences but took what was given him and never
made faces however bitter the medicine was. In
January he got well enough to get up and sit outside
on a bench and even to walk so far as the Cova and
pray there. Ti Marto would exclaim with pleasure
and encourage him; but the boy would simply look
thoughtful or say that it would not be long before our
Lady came. He said the same to his god-mother who

[1] Practically all the authors say that Francisco fell sick on December
23; but if this date is correct at all, it must refer to a relapse, because
already on All Saints' day, when it is the custom for children to come
round begging for apples and so forth, João, one of Marto's sons, had
to call out each time that no one could open the door because they
were all ill in bed.

'promised his weight in wheat' if he got better. However, not many days later he went to bed for good and all, but was so cheerful that they continued to hope against hope. At last he became so weak that he could not even say his rosary: he said to his mother that he could not pray because his head 'went round so'. Olimpia told him not to mind: he could pray in his heart and our Lady would understand just as well. But he became rapidly worse and could not eat; however, he said he wished to receive Holy Communion. Ti Marto went off to make arrangements with the priest, tormented by the strange anxiety lest the priest should again withhold the Blessed Sacrament from the dying boy, who might get muddled about some point in his 'catechism'. However, the priest agreed to come, and on the way Ti Marto, who had forgotten his beads, said the rosary on his fingers.

Meanwhile Francisco had asked that Lucia might be sent for and that he might see her alone. He wanted to know if she remembered any sins he had committed. She said he had sometimes been disobedient when his mother told him to stay at home, and had run away to be with Lucia or to hide. He said: 'Ask Jacinta.' Jacinta said that before our Lady appeared he had stolen a *tostao* (about a penny), and that when the Aljustrel boys threw stones at the Boleiros boys he threw some too. He agreed to all this; said he had confessed it already but would do so again; that he was terribly sorry and, should he not die, would never commit sins again. He added the prayer: 'Oh my Jesus, forgive us and deliver us from the fires of hell.' He asked Lucia to pray for him; she said she would but that our Lord had certainly forgiven him else our Lady would never have said that she was coming soon to fetch him to heaven.

The priest duly heard the boy's confession. Francisco begged his mother to give him nothing after midnight, so that he might be fasting 'like everybody else' for his Communion. April 3 dawned radiantly. When he heard the little bell heralding the Blessed Sacrament's approach, he tried to sit up but could not, and he received, lying down, his first and last Communion. When he re-opened his eyes, he said: 'When will you bring me the Hidden Jesus again?' But very soon there would be Communion without any veils.

Lucia remained with him all day. He whispered that he would miss her very much in heaven. She laughed and said that of course he wouldn't—in the company of our Lord and His Mother! He said: 'Yes; perhaps I had forgotten. . . .' When night fell, he was thirsty but could not drink the water they tried to give him. However, he said he was all right and had no pain. During the night he called his mother and said: ' Mother, look at that lovely light by the door.' After a little he said: 'Now I can't see it any more.' On April 4 he could still just speak, and begged his god-mother's pardon if he had hurt her in any way and asked her blessing. At 10 o'clock his face lit up and he smiled and then died without any effort.

Next day, the little procession started for Fatima —a cross, some men in green capes and the priest, and then four boys in white carrying Francisco's body, and then Lucia crying. Jacinta was too ill to come. It was Lucia who put up the simple wooden cross, like all the others in that humble cemetery; and thither she came daily to kneel beside her cousin's grave.

Such is the story of this little boy's life, in which, surely, is to be found no flaw: no word, no incident is untrue to character; and that character is not only innocent, but spiritual, and ever more spiritualised to the point, we may hope, of holiness. We are happy in that we can watch that growth which took its beginnings from the days spent not two years ago at the Cova da Iria: nor had he ever been 'disobedient to the heavenly vision', to which his own life is one of the strongest attestations.

Of course Jacinta's illness had been going on all this while, and much outlasted Francisco's. So long as Lucia could visit her little cousin, she did so and they would tell one another what 'sacrifices' they had been able to make—we recall that Jacinta had expressed her willingness to go on living entirely that she might make more sacrifices for sinners and save souls from hell.[1]

Lucia relates how her little cousin said that she never tired of telling our Lord and our Lady how she loved them—'I have a fire in my chest but it doesn't burn me'. Both she and Francisco asked Lucia to take the pieces of penitential cord and hide them lest their mother should see them and be upset. Lucia did so, but burnt them before she went away from Aljustrel.

Most of what we know about Jacinta during this period comes from Lucia, though it can be checked

---

[1] Lucia said to Fr. McGlynn (p. 74), that the children took it for granted that when our Lady asked for 'sacrifices' she meant 'voluntary sacrifices', i.e., over and above keeping the commandments; but in 1940 she again asked for penance and sacrifice, but those that were necessary for fulfilling religious duties and the duties of one's state. Fr. McGlynn asked if this were a mitigation of the former request and Lucia said that our Lady did not explain that to her. It will be remembered that there seems a slight confusion between the statement that they did not *seek out* special penances and the history of their periodical penitential acts, like not drinking, or using the sharp cord. My impression is that from time to time they did such acts, perhaps erratically and without judgement: as a rule their relatives saw no difference in them. We saw that quite possibly it was Fr. Faustino Ferreira who taught them a sort of 'ascetical discipline'.

here and there by what Ti Marto and Olimpia relate. Olimpia in fact said that it saddened them to see Jacinta lying hour after hour, her hands over her face, immovable. If asked what she was thinking about, she said: 'Nothing.' But she and Lucia would talk in whispers for hours on end and yet never would divulge what they had been saying. It would, in fact, be difficult to chronicle such fragments of her talk as survive, without too many repetitions: and after all the child was still a child, and very weak, and had but few words and was absorbed in but a few thoughts.

It is clear how much these children loved one another. Jacinta used to sit sadly on her bed and when asked what was the matter would say she was thinking of Francisco and how much she wanted to see him again. But Lucia herself has said that it was the thought of hell and saving sinners from it that almost obsessed the child.

'I am thinking of the war that will come: so many will die and go to hell! So many houses will be destroyed and priests killed. I am going to heaven soon but when you see the light our Lady told us of (see p. 159) you must come too.'

'But', said Lucia, 'one can't go to heaven just when one likes!'[1]

---

[1] It is difficult to be sure of what Jacinta said and when. Earlier books showed an astonishing laxity when 'quoting'. The first form in which (so far as I know) Jacinta's statement occurred was that nearly all who had died in the *first* war had gone to hell. Many were so shocked by this that they took no further interest in the story of Fatima. Doubtless this had been written before it was known that Lucia had foretold a second war; and the sentence printed above certainly refers to the future. In another form the word 'millions' was used. Fr. McGlynn (p. 97) said to Lucia point-blank: 'Jacinta is reported to have said of those who would die in war that nearly all of them would be lost. Did our Lady say this?' Lucia answered: 'I don't remember Jacinta's saying this. Our Lady never said anything about those dying in war going to hell. I don't know whether it was through revelation or intuition, but

Jacinta developed pneumonia and then a purulent abscess in her side which caused her real agony. The doctor decided that she must absolutely be taken to the hospital in Vila Nova de Ourém. Not only the idea of being separated from Lucia was dreadful to her, but she became convinced that the hospital would be perfectly dark and that she would not be able to see anything. But even the thought that she must suffer alone and in the dark gave her new material that she could use as expiatory sacrifice. Not, however, till July was Ti Marto able to take her, sitting on a donkey, to the hospital. Luckily the hospital was bright and cheerful and there were others in the ward; but her only days of real happiness during those two months were when Olimpia could bring Lucia to see her. But she maintained her interior happiness knowing that all the while she was fulfilling the vocation that had been granted her. After two months she was no better; the open wound suppurated worse and had to be dressed daily; but even so, she was brought back to Aljustrel as the doctors agreed they could do no more good and her parents could not afford a longer treatment.

When Canon Formigão visited her, he found her wasted away to a skeleton, for tuberculosis, too, was undermining such strength as was left to her. It is true that Jacinta used to try, says Lucia, to get up, prostrate herself, and say the 'Angel's prayer' (p. 145); but she simply fell over and had to say it on her

Jacinta had visions of people dead in the streets from war. Jacinta in horror said: "Can it be that most of these will go to hell?" This was her own reflection.' That is doubtless true; still, it shows the bent of the child's mind; and though we may up to a point regret it, we cannot but relate it to the vision spoken of on page 158. We recall that the whole life of St. Benedict Joseph Labre was dominated by the idea of the 'small number of the saved' which is in no sense a dogma of the Church nor a subject for revelation.

knees. Lucia soon enough asked Fr. Ferreira to assure
the child that she must simply say the prayer in bed,
which, with docility, she did. We are, then, disconcerted on learning that when winter came Jacinta's
parents 'no longer' allowed her to go to the Cova, but
did permit her to go to an occasional week-day Mass
at Fatima, if only to compensate for those who
didn't go even on Sundays. We may admit that fear
of infection was not the motive of this decision, but
rather, anxiety lest Jacinta should be harried by the
devout. We also recognise the almost unlimited
endurance of a peasant child; and Catholic countries
are less nerve-ridden than paganised ones are, and
the Portuguese uplanders are very sturdy. But it seems
to me that only a great deal of faith could have
induced Ti Marto and Olimpia to allow the child to
make these painful expeditions, and Jacinta herself
showed real heroism when making them.

It does not follow that the child found everything
—even small things—easy. She hated milk, and it
was only when Lucia reminded her that to eat the
milk-puddings she was given was a *sacrifice* that she
would take them. Now, if her mother brought her
grapes, she would take milk by preference. Lucia
could not receive Holy Communion every day; but
when she could, she at once visited Jacinta, who said
that though she could not see Him nor hear Him
she loved to have Him near her. 'If only I could go
to Communion in the church! Do you think one can
go to Communion in heaven?' Lucia gave her a
picture of the Sacred Heart. Jacinta did not like it.
Still, she kept it under her pillow till it was all
crumpled. 'I kiss His Heart', she said, 'it's what I like
best.' And she asked for one of the Heart of our Lady.
'I should like to keep the two together.' Lucia wrote
that Jacinta had begged her to make known God's

will that the Hearts of Jesus and Mary should be kept side by side.

Lucia relates that in December 1919, Jacinta told her she was to go to a second hospital in Lisbon, whence our Lady would come to take her to heaven. The child was torn between the joyous prospect of going to heaven and anguish at the thought of dying alone.

'But what does it matter', said Lucia, 'if our Lady is coming to fetch you?'

'Yes; it doesn't really matter, but sometimes I can hardly remember that she is coming for me.'

Jacinta's family regarded this notion of going to Lisbon as nonsense. The treatment at Ourém had done her no good and even there the fees had been too heavy. However, one day a motor-car arrived bringing Canon Formigão and a Dr. Eurico Lisboa and his wife. Jacinta's parents said that they could hardly regret her illness since all she wanted was to follow Francisco as soon as possible, and that it was useless to try to preserve her life. The doctor replied that no normal scientific means should be neglected, so as to make sure whether it really was our Lady's wish to take her. The Canon wholly agreed and it was arranged on the spot that she should go to one of the best Lisbon hospitals. Jacinta said she was in fine condition to go to Lisbon. . . Her father insisted that so it must be. She said that even if she recovered from this illness she would immediately get another. Going to Lisbon meant saying goodbye. . . . Well, she asked to be taken for the last time to the Cova and rode there on a friend's donkey. She could not have walked. At the Carreira pool she got off and said the rosary by herself and picked a few flowers for the chapel. At the Cova they knelt down and she prayed a little 'in her own way'. When they rose, Jacinta said:

'Mother, when our Lady went away she passed over those trees and afterwards she went into heaven so quickly that I thought her feet would get caught.'

Ti Marto had called on a friendly neighbour, Baron Alvaiazere, and told him that the journey was all settled; Olimpia and their son Antonio would accompany the child, and Antonio would tie a white handkerchief to his arm so that the ladies who were to meet them would recognise him. Ti Marto wrote (apparently to these ladies) explaining this and registered the letter. 'Oh, Senhor Marto'! exclaimed the post-official, 'what a lot of money you're spending!'

Marto explained to his wife that she must apologise to fellow-travellers—the child was very ill, which caused so unpleasant a smell: Jacinta was not to lean out when another train was passing . . . when they approached Lisbon and entered the Rossio tunnel they must not forget the handkerchief . . . and—she *must not worry*. . . . Poor Olimpia, who had never been in a train before! Lucia made her last visit to Jacinta, who repeated that they would meet no more.

Olimpia, Antonio and Jacinta went to the station in a mule-cart. Jacinta stood nearly all the time looking out of the window. At Santarém a lady offered her some sweets but she would not eat them. At Lisbon there was a—perhaps characteristic—moment of panic. Antonio, 'who knew how to read', went off to look at something—he was lost! No. He soon reappeared with three ladies who had come to fetch them. While Olimpia and Jacinta had been sitting in the waiting-room, a lady, a patient of Dr. Lisboa, came up and asked Jacinta to pray for her. The child simply looked sadly at her and said nothing. The lady left a 50-escudo note in her hand; she afterwards gave it to the superior of the house where she was and said: 'Keep it; I am going to give you a

lot of trouble.' She also said that she *had* prayed for
the lady but was in such pain that she said nothing
for fear of forgetting.

But a shock awaited them. No one wanted to
receive Olimpia and Jacinta into their house. Possibly
they had not realised how sick the poor child was.
They tramped around until they found a sort of
orphanage where a certain Mother Godinho acted as
'god-mother', *Madrinha*, to some twenty-five children.
She at last accepted Jacinta, and Olimpia too stayed
there for some time.[1]

Jacinta was very happy. The house adjoined the
chapel of Milagres and had a tribune looking down
upon the altar. Carried in the arms of Olimpia or
the Superior, she was able to receive Communion
daily.[2] She went to confession in the great Estrela
church hard by and exclaimed how good the priest
was—'He asked me so many things!' Olimpia was
devoured with curiosity about this, but knew she
mustn't enquire.

Very soon Jacinta made friends with the children,
one especially, to whom she gave naïf little sermons—
'with authority!' says Mother Godinho, who listened
at the half-open door. In some way she again saw our
Lady—'Move, please, dear Mother', she said: 'I am
waiting for our Lady.' 'It was not like at Fatima, but
I knew it was she', said the child.

During Jacinta's sojourn in this house, Mother
Godinho noted down many of her sayings, often

[1] This charitable lady had never, I am assured, been a nun, as is
usually said, but was leading a kind of 'lay religious' life.

[2] It is curious that the parish-priest of Fatima and Lucia both say
that Jacinta had never yet made her first Communion: Ti Marto said
she had, very devoutly: Mother Godinho evidently assumed she had:
Olimpia told us that she made it at six, which is impossible, but it is
not surprising if this very old lady, mother of so many, should have
grown confused about dates.

quoted as so profound as quite to outstrip the knowledge of an ignorant little girl. They do not seem so
to me; but allowing that Portuguese is a somewhat
magniloquent language and that children express
themselves in quite a 'formed' style, I think, too, that
we dare not judge what a phrase which to us might
seem very *simple* may have meant to Jacinta, whose
heart was purified as ours are not, nor in what words
she actually said it. Thus Jacinta would say—

'The sins of the world are very great. . . . If men
knew what eternity is they would do everything to
change their lives.'

'You must pray much for sinners and priests
and religious: priests should concern themselves only
with the things of the Church.'

'If the Government would leave the Church in
peace and give liberty to religion it would have God's
blessing.'

'Mother, fly from riches and luxury: love poverty
and silence; have charity even for bad people.'

'Confession is a sacrament of mercy and we must
confess with joy and trust.'

'Priests must be very pure. Disobedience of
priests and religious to their superiors gravely dis-
pleases our Lord. Pray for rulers.'

'Fashions will offend our Lord very much. People
who serve God should not follow the fashions. The
Church has no fashions. Our Lord does not change.'

'Many marriages are not of God and do not
please our Lord. The sins that cause most people to
go to hell are those of the flesh.'

'The Mother of God wants more virgin souls
bound by the vow of chastity.'

'I would gladly go into a convent but I would
rather go to heaven.'

'To be a religious one must be very pure in body
and mind.'

Mother Godinho said: 'Do you know what it is to be pure?'

'Yes, yes, I know. To be pure in body means to be chaste; to be pure in mind means not to commit sins, not to look at what one should not see, nor to steal or lie and always to tell the truth even if it is hard.'[1]

She also alluded to war. 'Our Lady said that the world is full of wars and dissensions. Wars are the punishment for sin.'

'Our Lady can no longer uphold the arm of her divine Son which will strike the world.[2] If people amend their lives our Lord will even now save the world, but if they do not, punishment will come.'

Mother Godinho says that this refers to an event of which Jacinta spoke in secret (though not as part of *the* secret) but which could now be mentioned. Jacinta said that our Lord was terribly outraged by the sins and crimes committed in Portugal and for this reason a terrible social cataclysm threatened the country and particularly the city of Lisbon. A civil war or communist revolution would be unchained accompanied by sacking and violence and devastation of all kinds. The capital would be turned into an image of hell.

I certainly do not say that Jacinta may not have had a direct 'revelation' about this, nor do I speculate why the prophecy has not been fulfilled so far, nor

[1] Despite the healthy upbringing proper to country-life such as Jacinta had been accustomed to, perhaps she did not understand quite all that she said. Olimpia recalls that at Aljustrel Jacinta said: 'Dear Mother, you must never eat meat on Fridays nor give it to me, because our Lady said that sins of the flesh bring many to hell.' *Carne* is the word that would have been used in each case; but Friday abstinence has nothing to do with sins of the flesh, and we cannot suppose that Jacinta was consciously making a sort of play on words.

[2] This sentence was a kind of refrain in our Lady's message at La Salette.

whether it still may be. She certainly seems to have
had what many would call 'second sight'.

Mother Godinho once asked Olimpia if she would
like her daughters Florinda and Teresa to become
nuns. Olimpia, who after all wanted someone to do
the household work, exclaimed in horror. Jacinta, who
had not heard this conversation, said afterwards: 'Our
Lady would like my sisters to become nuns, but my
mother would not like it: so our Lady will take them
to heaven before long.' The girls, in fact, died at 17
and 16 soon after Jacinta's own death.

She also told Mother Godinho, who had long
wished to visit the Cova, that she would do so, but only
after her, Jacinta's, death. And in fact she accompanied the child's coffin to Vila Nova de Ourém,
and thus was able, along with Lucia, to fulfil her
wish.

One of Jacinta's doctors asked her to pray for
him in heaven; she said she would, but that he would
follow her soon. To the other, she said the same, and
that his daughter would die too. All this happened
as foretold.

Again, she heard a sermon by a highly thought-of
priest, and said: 'That priest will turn out badly
though you wouldn't think it now.' And in fact he
soon enough apostatised and lived no more as a
priest.

She dictated a letter to Lucia saying our Lady
had predicted the day and hour of her death.

I have written the preceding paragraphs half
reluctantly, aware that to English readers some of
Jacinta's sayings may seem banal or even priggish.
As for banality, I have suggested above that a sentence
like 'God is good', 'Sin is terrible', may sound banal,
or a soul-shaking truth, according to the spiritual
receptivity of the hearer. Again, spoken as she spoke

them, I do not think they would have sounded banal to, for example, a Portuguese servant-girl who would have none of our sophistication. Anyhow, the poor child did not make all these remarks on end—they were not her entire conversation! Finally, they reach us filtered down through Mother Godinho (who will have used a conventional 'style'), and then Lucia; and we are in no way obliged to regard them all as due to direct divine illumination—when her 'god-mother' asked her how she knew all these things, she answered: 'Some our Lady tells me; others, I think for myself. I do love thinking!'

It seems strange that Dr. Lisboa, who had arranged for Jacinta to come to the city entirely that she might enter hospital, should not have ensured her, if not a bed there, at least a domicile, and rather hard that Mother Godinho should have been rebuked for admitting a tuberculous child into her own group. Anyhow, on February 2, Jacinta was admitted to the Estfania hospital, in the children's ward, and though Mother Godinho and other friends visited her daily, life became very desolate for her; doctors boasted of their unbelief and the nursing was deplorable. On February 10 she had two ribs removed; only a local anæsthetic could be used, so weak was she. The daily dressing of the vast wound that remained was agonising, but no one ever heard her complain. She was still fulfilling her vocation. However she told Mother Godinho that our Lady had appeared and told her she would soon fetch her, and also, take away the pain. Dr. Lisboa himself witnessed to the sudden disappearance of the pain and to Jacinta's being able to play about again. Here, too, she told Mother Godinho not to stand or sit in a particular place—that was where she had seen our Lady; and a nurse, who stood there on purpose, says that Jacinta's face 'took on such an expression of pain that I felt I could not remain there'.

Dr. Lisboa writes as follows: 'On the evening of February 20, at about 6 o'clock, Jacinta said she felt worse and wished to receive the Sacraments. The parish-priest, Dr. Pereira dos Reis, was called and heard her confession at about 8 that night. I was told that Jacinta had insisted that the Blessed Sacrament be brought to her as Viaticum, but that the priest had not agreed because she seemed fairly well. He promised to bring her Communion in the morning. Jacinta again asked for Viaticum, saying that she would shortly die, and indeed she died that night, peacefully, but without having received Communion. A young nurse, Aurora Gomes, was the only person present.'

In Portugal, burial must take place twenty-four hours after death; it was decided therefore that Jacinta's body should be taken next day, Sunday, to a Lisbon cemetery. But Dr. Lisboa thought that since the authenticity of the Apparitions might some day be recognised, the coffin had better be put in the parish church of the Angels till a vault could be found to receive it. Dr. Reis, however, demurred; still, owing to the intercession of some members of the Confraternity of the Blessed Sacrament, he allowed it to be placed on two stools in a corner of the sacristy.

Lisbon seemed to know in a moment that Jacinta had died, and people trooped to the sacristy to the grave annoyance of Dr. Reis. He feared a 'premature cultus' and also trouble with the sanitary authorities, since it had somehow been decided that Jacinta should be taken to the Alvaiazere vault at Vila Nova de Ourém, and this could not be managed before Tuesday. He began by locking the coffin up in an office and then took it up to the Confraternity room above the sacristy. He then handed over the key to Senhor Antonio Almeida, head of the undertaking firm which was to manage the funeral. This gentleman escorted groups of visitors to the room where Jacinta lay in her open coffin, and wrote afterwards that she seemed to be alive, with the loveliest colour, unlike anything he had ever seen; and not only no trace of the unpleasant odour due to her illness remained, but he and many others affirmed that to the very end a fragrance as of the most delicious flowers breathed round her. 'Not even the hardiest sceptic could doubt it.' At 11 a.m. on February 24 the body was placed in a leaden coffin, which was sealed and taken through the rain that afternoon to the station.

An episode related by Dr. Lisboa comes in startling contrast. The annual general meeting of the Conferences of St. Vincent de Paul was taking place in the presence of the Cardinal Patriarch and leading Catholics, clerical and lay. The doctor arrived late and explained that he had been at the funeral. Everyone burst into laughter, including the Cardinal. . . . So very far were almost all the clergy from believing in the Apparitions, let alone from organising the episode of Fatima. Not that they sank to the level of the anti-clericals, who accused the Catholics of murdering Francisco and Jacinta lest they should contradict Lucia or own up to fraud. . . .

Ti Marto and Baron Alvaiazere had heard that the operation was successful and Jacinta well. Some ten days later the Baron sent for Ti Marto and began by giving him some food. Then he pulled out a letter and read from it that 'Jacinta stood the operation well but they did something and she died'.

'Is there anything I must do?' asked her father.

'Nothing, Senhor Marto; nothing.'

After a few more days the Baron wrote that Marto

must go to Vila Nova de Ourém and bring the coffin to be placed in his vault. When Ti Marto saw it, he cried like a child. 'I have never cried so much. . . . I felt it had all been no good, all useless; she had been in the hospital two months here and then had gone to Lisbon and in the end she died all alone.'

Jacinta had said she would return to Fatima, but only after her death. So we may add, anticipating somewhat, that on September 12, 1935, the Bishop of Leiria decided to translate the bodies of the children to a tomb especially built at Fatima. The coffin was opened and Jacinta's face was seen to be perfectly incorrupt. It was photographed and a copy was sent to Lucia, who was in ecstasy at seeing her friend once more. She prayed that some day Jacinta might be canonised, and it was because of this photograph that she began to write the *mémoir* of Jacinta. The relics were first taken to the Cova, where the Bishop of Evora offered Mass, and then to Fatima, where they lie in the tomb described earlier, with its simple inscription:

'Here lie the mortal remains of Francisco and Jacinta to whom our Lady appeared.'

As for Lucia, she, too, was to disappear. In 1918 the ancient diocese of Leiria had been brought to life again, and Dr. José Alves Correia da Silva was consecrated bishop on July 25, 1920.[1] He soon enough saw that Lucia had better be removed from Aljustrel, not only to be freed from importunate questionings, but also to test whether visitors came to

[1] This Bishop, now old and infirm, was born near Braga in 1872. When the 'republic' was inaugurated in 1910, he was forcibly taken from his presbytery and made to stand in icy water for hours on end, which permanently crippled him. When he took up his charge as bishop, he found his diocese practically ruined, and his episcopal residence turned into barracks and government offices, and he had to find lodgings where best he could.

the district primarily from devotion or out of curiosity. He foresaw, too, that a canonical enquiry into the Apparitions would have to be set up, and it would be impossible seriously to examine Lucia at home. Her father had died, and Maria Rosa was not at all averse to her daughter's being sent to school at a distance where no one knew her. She took Lucia to see the bishop on June 13 and it was decided that she should leave on the 18th for the Dorothean Sisters' school at Vilar, near Oporto. In the school no one was to know who she was, nor must she speak of or be spoken to about the Apparitions. Indeed, no one must know that she was leaving, or when.

She spent her last day visiting the Cabeço and the Valinhos and thence went to the Cova and then to the parish church at Fatima, where she had been baptised and made her First Communion, and then knelt by her father's grave and Francisco's. When she came home, supper was not quite ready and she went down to the well where she had spent so long with her two cousins who had already gone to heaven as our Lady had said they would. At two next morning she went off with her mother and when they reached the Cova went down into it and said the rosary. Senhor Carreira accompanied them after that, and this part of her life was over.[1]

---

[1] Lucia after a while entered the Dorothean congregation as postulant at Tuy, just over the Spanish border, in 1925: next year she became a novice and in 1928 took her first vows as a lay-sister; in 1934 she took her final vows. Authority, anxious to make quite sure of various details connected with the Apparitions, sent her to Fatima in 1946: they must have felt very sure of the solidity of her character, since inevitably she became the centre of crowds of the devoutly curious. But having endured this publicity, she felt that her mission was accomplished and she was allowed to enter the Carmel of Coimbra as, it is said, she had wished from the outset to do. Her favourite saints are said to have been Ste. Thérèse de Lisieux and, interestingly, St. John Berchmans: she felt she could 'imitate *those*'.

Her disappearance caused much comment, some of it malicious. Was it, then, the ecclesiastics' turn to kidnap her? The Administrator sent for Maria Rosa, who answered curtly: 'My daughter is where she wishes to be, and where I wish.'[1] He let her go without more questioning.

[1] In my edition of Fonseca's Italian book we read, 'and *not* where I wish, but the 'not' is inked out.

CHAPTER 8

## END OF THE FIRST ACT

A SMALL chapel had, as we have said, been
hurriedly built but as yet no statue inhabited it.
A certain Gilberto had wished to contribute largely
to the chapel; when he found it finished he agreed to
help towards the making of a statue and went often
to question the children (this was before Jacinta left
for Lisbon) as to what it should look like. It was in
fact made, but since it was rumoured that the anti-
clericals meant to bomb the place it remained hidden
in the Fatima sacristy. It was hoped, however, to
bring it to the chapel on Ascension Day, 1920, when
a huge pilgrimage was being organised at Torres
Novas. This caused official indignation to blaze up
again. On April 24, 1920, Julio Bento (?) Ferreira (?)[1]
wrote to the Administrator of Vila Nova de Ourém
from *O Secretario Exterior*, as follows:

'Sir . . . it has come to our knowledge that reactionary elements in your county are preparing to
canonise (*sic*) the deceased seer of Fatima and so
continue the disgusting religious exploitation of the
people that has been set in motion. We beg you
therefore to inform us as to what stage these man-
oeuvres have reached in order that we, the Government, and your good self may take such precautions

[1] I have to say that the signature is doubtful because, presumably,
illegible; anyhow, after exhaustive enquiries kindly made for me in
official quarters, no such person seems known of; and what is more, no
meaning can be attached to *O Secretario Exterior*, unless it signifies a
Lisbon department concerned with outside-Lisbon affairs. It is supposed that during those chaotic years, almost anyone who wanted a
position (and some money) could have something created for him which
will have lasted as long as the ephemeral 'Government' then in power
did.

as may seem desirable to neutralise this shameless Jesuitical trick.'

Santos, in fact, swore that he would put a stop to this ridiculous fairy-tale. His secretary Julio Lopes said: 'You won't be able to do anything.' Santos replied: 'Not a soul shall get there. They can't do anything against force. I shall mobilise the whole artillery.' He interviewed all the regional officials, and on May 7 received a telegram from the civil governor of Santarém saying that H.E. the Minister of the Interior had decided that the Fatima mystification must not be repeated and that anyone responsible for organising a procession or other religious performance must be warned that disobedience would incur all the penalties laid down by law. Santos at once acted upon this but also asked for armed troops from Santarém. He received two more telegrams saying that the Municipal Guard, under arms, would occupy strategic points and prevent any access to Fatima.

Canon Formigão writes that despite alarming rumours that prevented many who had intended to accompany him, he determined to try and reach Fatima and arrived very early on May 13 at Vila Nova de Ourém in pouring rain and thunder. Cavalry galloped by; machine-guns were expected. It was said that no one would be allowed to go to Fatima, and numbers of farm-carts whose owners had hoped for a profitable day were—to their great annoyance, republican or not—countermanded. Then it was said that people might go to Fatima but no further. Yet an interminable stream of vehicles filled with laughing pilgrims kept going past. The Administrator was seen, moving around, smiling uncomfortably. Then he was seen in a car, escorted by men with rifles. The Canon got through to Fatima where the

134 THE MEANING OF FATIMA

approaches were absolutely choked with cars; up to midday, he was told, everyone got as far as the Cova, but then the Administrator arrived and prevented others from doing so. Still, many struggled through across the fields. The Fatima church was packed: Fr. Cruz was preaching and saying the rosary. A doctor, outside, was explaining to the people that the Cova was being turned into a regular fair; that our Lady would not have liked this—what she asked was prayer and penance—the authorities were, in fact, carrying out her wishes. A riot seemed imminent—a man tried to break through and the Guard began to deal out blows right and left. The Canon persuaded the peasants to obey orders—there was merit in that. One of the guards told the Canon how he hated his duty—he was religious himself—Our Lady of Fatima had saved his sister's life. . . . At last the Canon decided to return, along with a crowd of others, soaked but joyous. Meanwhile a business-man, though apparently a republican, was railing at the Administrator for a fool—he was preventing the progress of the country-side; how much money the coachmen from surrounding towns must have lost! It would have been new for Sr. Santos to hear himself called the enemy of Progress!

He received, however, the most effusive congratulations. Thus the Portuguese Federation of Free Thought wrote to thank him for his action, so loftily republican and free-thinking, which he had taken in regard of the pretended miracle of Fatima whereby Jesuit and clerical reaction were trying to exploit popular ignorance. Santos threw bouquets back, alluding to the complete reverse suffered by reaction; the bringing to nothing of the projected procession, and of the new hateful attack that was being prepared against the Republic.

'However', said he, 'these authentic enemies of the Republic and promoters of Fatima are not yet disarmed, since they propose to transfer with all their ceremonial the body of a wretched child who died in Lisbon and whom they consider the "intermediary" of the Virgin, to another tomb. And they also make use of the so-called seer, Lucia of Jesus, a child of 13, a poor and sickly girl, the better to exploit the ignorant people. But such pitiable projects must fail of their effect while a Government such as we now have and associations such as the Federation of Free Thought fulfil their august mission, which is, to combat lies and to defend liberty.'

It was, then, thought prudent not to bring the statue to its niche, and the curious device of *veiling* the niche was thought of, so that people should feel as if it were there. Finally it was brought to the Cova, but again they heard rumours that the place would be bombed, so every night it was carried to Maria (Carreira) da Capelinha's house till the morning. And indeed during the night of March 6, 1922, fanatics exploded four bombs in the chapel and blew the roof away; another, by the stump of our Lady's tree, failed to go off. The bishop forbade the rebuilding of the chapel for the time being; however, it was not long before the people determined to bring back the statue from Maria's house where our Lady was ceaselessly venerated; everyone wanted a share in carrying it, so small groups each took it a yard or two. It was from this time that the practice grew up of taking away a little earth from the Cova, mingling it with water, and drinking it. Many graces, thus obtained, were recorded.

Undeterred by the dynamiting of the chapel, the Bishop of Leiria that same year (May 3, 1922) made a preliminary statement concerning the events at

Cova da Iria and set up a commission to make a canonical enquiry into them. On October 12, 1926, he made his first visit to the shrine, where the throngs of pilgrims had continuously increased. He observed at once the distressing lack of water—not a spring, not a real well, in the whole district. It was a certain Sr. José Alves who persuaded a beginning to be made by digging in the middle of the great depression, for even in dry weather there was a little water there and a few reeds. Almost at once they reached rock. They proceeded to blast downwards and suddenly water gushed up. The well, however, was not finished, yet people came in multitudes to drink the water, still, it would seem, earthy; and they would carry it off in all sorts of vessels. It was not long before the Administrator of Ourém (by now, Antonio Pavilon) wrote to an official at Fatima that it had been brought to his notice that an open ditch of water had been dug to which people suffering from, diseases both interior and exterior resorted. It must at once be covered as being an immediate danger to public hygiene. Since no one was likely to do this, the Administrator, together with the Sub-delegate of Public Health, visited the place and called on the parish-priest and said that the whole thing was disgusting and a disgrace to the parish. They repeated that the 'well' must be covered, or he must accept all responsibility.

Next year still nothing had been done; after another letter to authority had described the well as full of filth and microbes and a menace to public health and sanitation, the bishop caused it to be covered, whereupon the Sub-delegate declared the water drinkable and the central edifice was built surmounted in due course by a pillar and a gilt statue of the Sacred Heart. It was surrounded by a wide verandah beneath which the water could be obtained through fifteen taps, especially when a second spring flowed forth somewhat later. This edifice is now in part demolished owing to the transformation that the Cova is undergoing; the water, however, is still collected in a vast cistern underground.

The first part of the history of Fatima is therefore fully over; in fact, it was finished when Francisco and Jacinta had died and Lucia had disappeared from the scene. So far, the Message given by our Lady at the Cova had been concerned wholly with repentance, and the saying of the rosary. Even the miracle of the sun ceased to play any central part in popular imagination, and certainly it is not from that that we are to learn what our Lady wanted from that generation or from ourselves. But contained within this period is the transformation of the lives of Francisco and Jacinta; this, it seems to me, is the first great miracle which would be an effect without a cause were the Apparitions themselves not authentic.

The character of Lucia will reveal itself somewhat as we follow her career; but in any case it would be ill-becoming to say much about one who is still alive. Before the other two, however, we may well be on our knees—the sturdy little boy, who liked hunting snakes and who played so gaily on his pipe, and who became a true little mystic, absorbed by the thought of consoling God, and of the hidden Presence of our Lord; the sensitive little girl, so good at dancing, so fond of singing, who was asked to suffer so terribly, and did so, so gladly, if but she might rescue sinners from the 'enduring consequences' of their sin.

It is with real regret that I must say goodbye to the harsh sunlight and the torrential rains that beat remorselessly on the stony Serra with its black-green metallic trees, where these two brief lives were lifted from innocence into holiness.

## PART II

## 1925-1941: VEILS BEGIN TO LIFT

FOR a long time this was all that the general
public knew about 'Fatima'; I think that even
the hope of learning what the 'secret' was, was given
up. But gradually a few persons became aware that
Lucia declared that she was still receiving com-
munications from our Lady. Letters were written by
her, some of which presumably have ceased to exist
while others are in private hands or perhaps by now
in the episcopal archives. What reached the public,
little by little, were the documents written in 1936-
1937 and above all in 1941-1942. It was when she
sent the last-mentioned to the bishop that she wrote
to him on December 8, 1941:

'I think, my Lord, that I have written everything
which up to now Your Lordship has ordered me to
write. Hitherto I had done all I could to hide the
most intimate parts of the Apparitions of our Lady at
Cova da Iria. Every time I was obliged to speak of
them I tried to touch on them very lightly, indeed,
not to unveil what I so much wanted to keep hidden.
But now that obedience obliges me to—here it is!
And I remain like a skeleton, stripped of everything,
of life itself, and placed in a museum, to remind the
visitor of the misery and nothingness of all passing
things. . . . May the good God and the Immaculate
Heart of Mary deign to accept the poor sacrifices
that they have deigned to ask of me, in order to

revive in souls the spirit of faith, of confidence and of love.'

It will be seen that she has formed, so to say, a 'style', part personal and part 'conventual', and though 'style' as such does not affect the substance of her narrative, I think it is a pity to weave what she said *in* that style into the sentences spoken by her when a very little girl, and quite incapable of speaking in any such way. But since she will constantly refer back to those earliest experiences, I too shall be, as I said, involved in many repetitions and must ask to be forgiven for this.

It may be remembered that during the first Apparition our Lady asked the children to return to the Cova for six months in succession, and often repeated this. Then she added: 'and I will come back here (*aqui*) a seventh time.' But later (pp. 91, 93) Lucia said that our Lady had not mentioned returning there any more and that she herself did not intend to go back to the Cova, while Jacinta said that on October 13 and earlier our Lady declared that that was the last time she would come. We must therefore assume that the word 'here' was a mistake on Lucia's part, made the more easily because she had no idea that our Lady was to appear to her anywhere else. The first intimation of any further vision refers to one on December 10, 1925 when, she relates, our Lady appeared to her in her convent, showing her 'heart ringed with thorns'.[1] Our Lady said:

[1] Lest a mistaken imaginative picture be formed of this, we may at once recall that Fr. McGlynn made his statue under the minute personal direction of Lucia, and shows the heart on a sort of disc and en-haloed by a ring of thorns (not wreathed with thorns, as the Sacred Heart of our Lord is normally represented). Some of these thorns project outwards; others pierce the heart itself. The figure was (as usual, we shall see) entirely of light: only the thorns appeared brown and burnt. The heart seemed to be about two inches in front of the left breast, which,

'Behold, my daughter, my Heart surrounded with the thorns with which ungrateful men continually pierce it by their blasphemies and ingratitudes. Do you at least try to console me, and for my part I declare to you that I promise to assist at the hour of death with the graces necessary to salvation all those who on the first Saturday of five consecutive months shall go to confession, receive Holy Communion, say five decades of the rosary and keep me company during a quarter of an hour, meditating the mysteries of the rosary with the intention of offering reparation to me.'

When it was suggested to Lucia that this was an almost verbal echo of the 'Great Promise' made to St. Margaret Mary, she answered bluntly that it was not for her to teach our Lady what to say.

She writes that from then on she tried to propagate the devotion of the Reparatory Communion with confession on five consecutive first Saturdays of the month and the recital of the rosary with a quarter of an hour's meditation; it is not quite clear whether this meditation was that which ought to be made while the rosary is recited, or supplementary. From a letter to her mother in which she says that this devotion is easy, it would seem that she regarded the 'meditation' on each mystery while it was being said as what she intended. She also asked her to make an act of reparation to our Lady for the offences she received from her ungrateful children and to try to persuade all whom she could to do the same. This letter was written on July 24, 1927.

She seems at this time to have had no regular 'director', but mentioned what she wanted to her actual confessor, a Fr. Lino, and to her Superior,

as Fr. McGlynn says, was difficult to portray in sculpture. The left hand was not holding the heart, but some distance below it. The right hand was raised, but not pointing to the heart.

who advised her to write to her previous confessor at
Oporto, Mgr. Pereira Lopes, but he did not reply.
Her Superior then suggested her writing to a Fr.
Francisco Rodrigues, S.J., then at Pontevedra.

Writing to Fr. McGlynn, she speaks as though the
request for the reparatory Communions was made in
1926, but also mentions 1925 and 1927: I presume
that the request was made several times with greater
or less detail. Anyhow, in 1926 she spoke of this to
her then confessor, Fr. José da Silva Aparicio, S.J.,
who afterwards went to Brazil. At that time, she
wrote, our Lady had not made her demand for the
consecration of Russia to the Immaculate Heart of
Mary; this occurred in 1929; at least, that is when,
she says, she wrote about it.

In 1927 (though it is far from easy to make quite
sure about actual dates) she was told by her confessor to say all that she could remember and was
permitted to say about her experiences. She asked
our Lord how she could obey her confessor without
disobeying our Lady's prohibition of the transmission
of a 'secret'. She heard His voice from the Tabernacle
clearly saying that she should say everything about
'this devotion' (i.e. to the Immaculate Heart; none
other was ever in question) except the 'secret'. Others
seem to place this event just ten years later, which
seems to me more likely. However, sooner or later she
drafted a letter to the Holy Father in which she said
that our Lady wished the Holy Father to consecrate
Russia to the Immaculate Heart, along with all the
bishops of the world on one and the selfsame day.
Lucia told two other priests about this, the latter of
whom undertook to see that her written request
reached the attention of Pius XI and he afterwards
informed Lucia that it had indeed been received by
the Pope and would be taken into consideration.

It seems right to recall that at least since the end
of the First World War many committees had peti-
tioned the Holy See to consecrate the world to the
Immaculate Heart (though no mention had been
made, so far as I know, of Russia as such);[1] and
secondly, that the Holy See was being positively
deluged by prophecies and 'revelations' from persons
of greater or less repute for holiness, and that up to
that time Lucia's request could hardly have been
viewed save as one among very many. A draft letter
certainly contains Lucia's rather startling request
(the mobilisation of *all* the bishops, and the request
that they should perform the consecration on *one*
definite day, would have meant an enormous amount
of work . . .); but Fr. McGlynn says the Cardinal
Patriarch recalls a copy of the letter but not this
special request. I hazard the conjecture that since it
is most improbable that Lucia's letters to the Pope,
written in her own unformed script, and on exercise-
book paper, were those which were actually sent,
those who were ultimately responsible for sending
them may well have omitted what they thought would
sound exorbitant. Even now, passages from her documents are not published for 'prudential' reasons (see
pp. 2 and 161). I repeat, this is a conjecture supported
by no positive evidence. Anyhow, Pius XI did not
accede to her request nor even to the much simpler
ones made by various hierarchies.

It is certain, at any rate, that in 1936 Lucia was
told by her confessor to write down what she could,
and after consulting our Lord and receiving the injunction mentioned above, she wrote two fascicules,
the second of which included the mention of an

[1] As from 1900-1914 seven petitions at least, signed by many
bishops, and every Marian Congress, had sent such a petition to Rome
(see Fonseca, p. 284).

angelic apparition, briefly touched upon in the previous document about Jacinta (the photograph of whose incorrupt face she had just received), though at first it was thought unwise to publish this. Finally, as the silver jubilee of the Apparitions approached, at the bishop's order she produced her two remaining documents (apart from the letter to be opened only in 1960), all, naturally, in the diction which by now was habitual to her. However, already in 1940 she had written to the bishop lamenting that the consecration had not been carried out as she had asked; and now, by order of her spiritual directors, she wrote to the Holy Father begging that the *world* might be consecrated to the Immaculate Heart, 'with special mention of Russia'. This is, in fact, what Pius XII did in 1943. It is these latter documents that we now can utilise; and if I myself, in what has been written above, have been guilty of unnecessary confusion, I can but hope it is not altogether my fault.

\*       \*       \*

Canon Formigão, we recall, returned on October 19, 1917, to Aljustrel, partly because he was upset by Maria Rosa's having told him that the previous year Lucia and three little companions (now known to have been Maria and Teresa Matias and Maria Justino) had seen what Lucia called a *vulto*, a sort of 'shape', enveloped in a sheet. This advanced towards the children and then retreated. It reappeared twice more; and though at that time Lucia did not know how to reckon in months, it seems to have appeared between the spring and the autumn of that year. When the Canon asked her why she had not told him about this before, she said it was 'nothing', and that she 'thought she had run away'. In later years she described this as a 'sort of cloud, whiter than snow, transparent, and in human form'. She also said that the impression made was one of 'alarm, bewilderment, and joy', but that it faded away and they might easily have forgotten it.

Now we hear that in the spring of 1916 Lucia, Jacinta and Francisco went with their sheep to a property of their parents at the bottom of the hill Cabeço called Chousa Velha. During the morning it began to drizzle and they climbed the hill to take shelter under a rock. This was in an olive-grove belonging to her god-father Anastacio, though it extended to a considerable distance and belonged to other persons too. The rain stopped, but the children went on playing there, had their lunch and said the rosary. By then the sun was shining and the day was clear. Suddenly a wind shook the trees.[1] They looked up, and saw in the distance over the trees to the east 'a light whiter than snow in the form of a young man, transparent and bright as crystal shone through by the rays of the sun'. He approached, and they began to discern his features, but they were so over-whelmed that they could say nothing. He said:

'Do not be afraid. I am the Angel of Peace. Pray with me.'

He then prostrated himself head to the ground and said:

'My God, I believe, I adore, I hope and I love Thee. I ask forgiveness for those who do not believe nor adore nor hope nor love Thee.'

He said this three times, the children repeating his words. Then he rose and said:

'Pray like that. The Hearts of Jesus and Mary are attentive to the voice of your supplications.'

---

[1] At Lourdes, before the first apparition St. Bernadette heard a strong wind, but observed that the poplars in the hard-by meadows were not stirring.

Then he disappeared, Lucia wrote that the impression left upon them was so profound at first that they remained in the same position for a long time repeating the prayer, and that the atmosphere of the supernatural was so strong that they could not say one word to one another about what had happened, still less to anyone else, though it never occurred to them to promise secrecy.

'It was so intimate that it was not easy to say the least word about it. It made all the greater impression because it was the first (apparition) that was so clear.'

None the less, the impression wore off; the children sang and danced as before, though they increasingly liked to be together and away from other children.

Summer came and the flocks were taken out early or in the evening. During the heat of the day the children played or rested under the fig-trees and by the well in the garden. It was here that the Angel appeared the second time. He said:

'What are you doing? Pray! pray much! The Hearts of Jesus and Mary have designs of mercy upon you. Constantly offer prayers and sacrifices to the Most High.'

'How are we to sacrifice?' said Lucia.

'In every way you can, offer a sacrifice to the Lord as an act of reparation for the sins by which He is offended and for the conversion of sinners. Thus you will draw down peace for our fatherland. I am the Angel who guards it, the Angel of Portugal. Above all, accept and bear with submission the suffering that the Lord is sending you.'

Francisco, meanwhile, had heard no words—he never did. He asked Lucia what the Angel had said. She (though they had begun to play again) was still so much under the impression of the apparition that she told him to wait till the next day or to ask Jacinta. But Jacinta too said that she would tell him tomorrow—'Today I can't talk.'

Next day, Lucia says, Francisco asked her if she had slept; he had not; he had been thinking about the Angel and what he could have said. She told him, but he began to ask questions:

'What is the Most High? What does it mean—the Hearts of Jesus and Mary are attentive to your supplications?'

She explained this, and he kept quiet and thoughtful before asking anything more. But, says she, 'my spirit was not free yet', and she again told him to wait till next day. Soon enough he ran off to Jacinta, who cried out:

'Keep quiet! one shou'dn't talk much about such things.'

Lucia writes that they all had an inexplicable feeling when speaking of the Angel; Jacinta said she could not play or sing and had no strength for anything. The boy said:

'It doesn't matter. The Angel is better than all that. Let us think of him!'

Lucia writes: 'The Angel's words were like a light which made us understand who God is, how He loves us and wishes to be loved; the value of sacrifice and how pleasing it is to Him and how it can convert sinners. So from that moment we began to offer to God everything that mortified us without, however, seeking out new mortifications or penances, except that we passed hours on end prostrate on the ground repeating the prayer that the Angel had taught us.'

When autumn came, one day when the children had taken their sheep out in the direction of Chousa Velha, the Angel reappeared, this time holding a chalice with a Host above it from which drops of blood fell into the cup. He left these suspended in the air, prostrated himself on the ground and said three times:

'Most Holy Trinity, Father, Son and Holy Ghost, I adore You profoundly and I offer You the most precious Body, Blood, Soul and Divinity of Jesus Christ, present in all the tabernacles of the world, in reparation for the outrages, sacrileges and indifference by which He is offended. And by the infinite merits of His most Sacred Heart and of the Immaculate Heart of Mary I beg You for the conversion of poor sinners.'

He then rose, gave the Host to Lucia and the chalice to the other two, saying:

'Take and drink the Body and Blood of Jesus Christ horribly outraged by ungrateful men. Make reparation for their crimes and console your God.'

He again prostrated himself, repeated three times the prayer 'Most Holy Trinity', and disappeared.

Francisco said to Lucia: 'The Angel gave you Communion but what did he give to Jacinta and me'?

'It was Holy Communion too. Didn't you see the Blood dripping from the Host?'

'I knew it was God in me', he said, 'but I didn't know how.'

Lucia writes that these Apparitions left them quite prostrate: 'I don't know why, but the Apparitions of our Lady produced quite different effects in us. We felt the same intimate happiness, the same peace and joy, but instead of physical prostration, an expansion of movement; instead of this annihilation in the divine presence, a desire to exult with joy; there was no difficulty of speech but rather a desire of communication. All the same, we felt also the need for silence especially about certain things.'

This narrative has suggested difficulties of various

sorts, due to different points of view. It is, of course, regretted that it comes from one source only and cannot be 'checked' by anyone else's information, as, for instance, the last days of Francisco can. Theologians have suggested that the offering of the Divinity of our Lord to the Holy Trinity is at least an 'innovation' in the Church's diction. Fr. Jongen (De Marchi, p. 307), to whom Lucia was insisting that the words of the prayer were accurate, asked if she couldn't possibly be mistaken. Lucia smiled and said: 'Perhaps the Angel made a mistake.' For my part, since the words were not audible to the ear, I am inclined to agree that Lucia, who knew from her catechism the phrase in which our Lord's *presence* in the Blessed Sacrament is expressed, used it quite naturally to interpret the Angel's injunction to *offer* our Lord, true God and true man, 'just as He is', in expiation. It has been asked, too, what the two little children made of Communion under the species of wine; and even if they knew very little about Holy Communion itself, they will have known that it must be received fasting. In any case, neither of them regarded this event as their 'First Communion'; Francisco made his on his death-bed; it is not clear when Jacinta made hers, but it was certainly a considerable time after this. We will be right, then, in regarding this Communion as a mystical and symbolic one; that is, that the children were made to feel most closely united with our Lord, and that they clothed their experience in imagery with which they were familiar; for the chalice with the Sacred Host above it is a very frequent *motif* in pious prints.

It has also been urged that we cannot accurately speak of 'the infinite merits of the Sacred Heart of our Lord and of the Immaculate Heart of our Lady', and in fact authors usually alter the sentence a little

—e.g. 'by the intervention of the Immaculate Heart' (Barthas): 'by the intercession of . . .' (Fonseca); but again, it is surely unnecessary to suppose that Lucia must have translated what she 'heard' into technically accurate phraseology. Nor need we dwell on expressions like the 'hours on end' during which Lucia says they remained prostrate repeating the angelic prayer; duration of time means little to a childish mind; nor on turns of phrase such as 'have merciful designs on you . . .'; there is no difficulty in supposing that Lucia as time went on put into adult phrases what she had heard, as a child, in her heart. As for the Angel's statement that he was the 'Angel of Portugal', the book of Daniel warrants our assuming that angels may have nationalities as well as individual souls in their charge; and the breviary addresses St. Michael as 'Angel of Peace'.

A really substantial problem seems to me to be offered by the story of the 'sheeted form'. Maria Rosa told Canon Formigão that this triple apparition of a sort of white silhouette, advancing and returning, occurred 'last year', i.e. 1916; Lucia did not contradict her, though it was not she who told her mother about it but, apparently, it was one of her little companions who made it known, and in one case it became talked of as a 'woman without a head'. Lucia herself said: 'I think I ran away.'

We have, it seems to me, three possibilities before us. Either between spring and autumn of 1916 Lucia saw the triple apparition of a sort of ghost, was frightened by it, but spoke about it when questioned, and *also* the triple apparition of the Angel but said nothing about it at all. Or else, we must assume that both Maria Rosa and Lucia were mistaken by a year about the spectral apparition and that it really happened in 1915, though I cannot see that this theory (now largely accepted) was mentioned till the angelic apparitions came up for discussion. In either case, the 'sheeted form' would remain enigmatic, since it seems to have no religious significance. Or finally we may suppose that the triple apparitions were in fact identical, and that Lucia simply had no words, or even clear ideas in which to describe her earlier experiences. This implies that there was much more to say about the 'sheeted form' than she *could* say at the time, and that, as time went on, she 'stylised' her account of the Angel and of the children's interior states not a little, which, so far as mere words go, she evidently did. Against this must be set the fact that when she saw the first, at any rate, of the spectral apparitions she was with three little girls and not with her cousins at all. Her statement about the exhaustion induced by the angelic apparitions—that they were the first to be so clear (*assim manifesta*)— may mean either that she had seen something else before which was more vague, or, that they were the first of a series of 'clear' apparitions (those of our Lady) which she was to see later.

Nobody can say *how* a pure spirit, such as an angel, can manifest itself to body-soul creatures such as we are; but it remains true that any such spiritual visitation has to be put into wholly human language by the person 'visited', and I am quite content to suppose that Lucia's latest statements which arrived, they say, 'like a bombshell' into the popular awareness, were the best description that she, after a long interval, could make of God's wonderful gift given, through His messenger, to her childhood.

*       *       *

Naturally, as time went on, Lucia amplified her original description of the Apparitions not a little.

Thus she finally described our Lady as 'brighter than
the sun, radiating a light more clear and intense than
a crystal cup filled with sparkling water lit by blazing
sunlight'. When the Lady said: 'You will have much
to suffer, but the grace of God will be your strength,'
she 'opened her hands and bathed us in a very intense
light which was like a reflection coming from them
and which penetrated our hearts and our intimate
souls so that we saw ourselves in God, who was this
light, more clearly than in a mirror. Then by an
impulse which was also interiorly given, we fell on
our knees and repeated inwardly: "O Holy Trinity,
I adore You. My God, my God, I love You in the
Blessed Sacrament."' Finally, the Lady 'began to rise
serenely, moving towards the east till she disappeared
in the immensity of space, surrounded by a vivid light
which seemed to open a path for her'.

Some may be inclined to prefer the simple version
originally spoken by the children to this literary, even
rhetorical, account; but it is evident that from the
outset 'light' was a keyword in their descriptions. It
may, then, be in place here to write what Lucia ultimately said about our Lady's appearance and dress.
Already in Fr. da Fonseca's book we find her saying:

'If I knew how to paint (and even if I did, I
would not be able to paint her as she is, because I
know that is impossible, just as it is impossible for
me to do it in words), I would put only a simple
dress, as white as possible, and a mantle hanging
from the head to the hem of the dress; and just as I
could not paint its light nor the beauty diffused
around it, I would suppress all the other adornments
except a delicate thread of gold around the mantle.
This "thread" stood out like a ray of sunlight shining
more brightly. The *comparison bears no relation to the
reality*, but I cannot express myself better.'

But much the fullest account of what Lucia thought and said is to be found in Fr. McGlynn's book where he tells how Lucia herself supervised his statue, as he modelled it, in the minutest detail. She described the Lady as 'all of light'. The tunic and the mantle were distinguishable as two 'waves of light' one above the other; the dress hung straight and was not precisely in folds, but the light 'undulated' and gave the impression of folds; she was very insistent that the poor sculptor must make 'folds' yet not realistic ones; they must give the effect of vibrant light. He therefore 'moved the tool rapidly from side to side with each downward stroke. The action resulted in a basically straight line broken with slightly scooped and concave forms.' Lucia said that this would do 'very well', insisting, however, that the dress must be drawn in slightly at the waist yet without any girdle and the folds below the waist must *not* correspond with those above it—a convex above must become concave below. The more she tried to express herself in terms of light, the more obstinately she made him produce something material. Thus the gold edging to the mantle was simply an intenser light and so was the cord hanging from the neck and joined by a little 'ball of light', and what she, as a child, had called 'earrings' were also a more vivid light. Fr. McGlynn thought to baffle her by asking: 'Did her face or hands have the colour of light or of flesh?' and was himself baffled when she replied: 'Flesh-like light' (*carnea luz*). 'She was all of light. The light had various tones, yellow, white and other colours. It was by the different tones and different intensities that one saw what was hand and what was mantle, what was face and what was tunic.'

She could not remember how many points the star displayed; but it, like the cord, was yellow,

not golden; she could not remember whether the
Lady had shoes or sandals—'I think I never looked
at the feet'. Still, she was very definite about details
of attitude and so forth; her first remark on seeing
Fr. McGlynn's original design was: 'It doesn't give
the position.' She kept making him alter the position
of the hands, the star, the 'ball of light' by fractions
of an inch; she kept telling him to make the mouth
smaller and then to lift it higher. The Sister who was
her companion rather surprisingly told him not to
worry: 'Your ideas of beauty may be just as good as
hers!' As for Lucia, she rightly declared that 'No
matter what you do, you won't give the impression
of the reality.'[1]

[1] Bishop Ullathorne, in his *Holy Mountain of La Salette*, written after
his pilgrimage there in 1854, says of the apparition there (pp. 48-49):
'The incessant agitation of enquiry has brought about a development
in the description of the apparition. The children have learnt French,
and have, with time, and the expansion of their minds, acquired an
accumulation of ideas and images, as instruments with which to convey
more perfectly what has always remained pictured within them, as it
were with light upon their souls. Criticism will remark upon the more
spiritualised form which the vision takes with these later explanations:
but then it should be recollected that while the words they heard were
not their own, and have no analogy with their characters, the descriptions of the vision emanate from themselves; and at first their minds
were rude and their own speech imperfect. . . . The restlessness of
Maximin made him less able to endure the exceeding brightness, and
hence he could not look into the face of "the Lady", but only saw the
head-dress and the form from beneath the face (which was) too dazzling
for him to bear. . . . (The children) describe the light which they first
saw as *incomparably brighter than the sun* . . . "there is no colour in the world
at all resembling it". In describing "the Lady" the only ideas they can
use are those of form, light and colour. (But whenever they use a
material word, even colour) they draw back, and say it was like no
earthly colour. What they call "roses", they instantly say were *not* roses.
. . . The head-dress is a "cap", but when questioned more, Mélanie can
give no other idea of any other substance in it than light, as it were
formed by streams of brilliancy.' The Lady (p. 52) produced a light
still more brilliant than the light which preceded her. When it was
alleged that there were slight discrepancies between the accounts of
the children, or within Maximin's own, the Bishop says (p. 91): 'I need

I return now to the document which contains Lucia's final account of the visions. On June 13, after the Lady had said she would leave her on earth for some time, we now read that she added:

'Jesus wishes to use you to make me known and loved. He wishes to establish in the world the devotion to my Immaculate Heart.'

'Must I stay here alone?'

'No, my child; do not be sad because of this. My Immaculate Heart will be your refuge and the way that will lead you to God.'

'It was at that moment', writes Lucia, 'that our Lady opened her hands and communicated to us once again the great light in which she was surrounded. In it we saw ourselves as it were submerged in God. Jacinta and Francisco seemed to be in that part of the light which went up to God and I in the part that was poured out over the earth. In front of the palm of our Lady's right hand was a Heart encircled with thorns that pierced it. We understood that it was the Immaculate Heart of Mary, outraged by the sins of humanity, and asking that they be made reparation for.'[1]

We recall that on December 17, 1927, Lucia asked our Lord how she could obey her confessor by writing down the graces she had received if among them was the 'secret of our Lady', she heard Him say:

scarcely allude to that widely received theory which maintains that even the prophets and apostles, when they record exterior, sensible and obvious facts amidst their revelations, do not receive such facts from direct inspiration, but are simply preserved from error [i.e. doctrinal or moral] in narrating them. Nor need I cite [he quotes the ordinary authorities] to show that true revelations, even revelations approved by the Church, are not always without some mixture in their narration of things unrevealed, or even untrue, so be it in a manner that does not affect the sense and bearing of the revelation itself.'

[1] Lucia, when explaining to Fr. McGlynn how to make his statue, caused him to put the Heart well *above* the *left* hand.

'Write what your confessor tells you to; write also all that the Blessed Virgin revealed in the Apparitions which refers to the devotion to her Immaculate Heart. Continue to hide the rest of the secret.'

Our Lady, in June, 1917, did not command the children to keep this subject a secret, but they felt an imperious need of doing so, and in fact thenceforward freely admitted that the Lady had told them *a* secret. But what became known as *the* secret was reserved for July 13. It was, therefore, ten (or twenty) years later that Lucia saw a vision already seen, she felt, in 1917.

I must here allude to what has been a difficulty for many. It is equally obvious that at first the children did not know who was appearing to them; that in a very short time they felt sure it was our Lady; and that everyone who believed in the Apparitions at all assumed it *was* our Lady. It is also certain that Lucia constantly asked: 'Who are you and what do you want?' and that the Lady said she would tell them who she was and what she wanted *only* on October 13 (Canon Barthas omits the 'only', see p. 66). But if from the very outset the Apparition had spoken of her Immaculate Heart and was to continue to do so and evidently expected to be understood, how could the children have had any doubt as to who the Lady was?[1] It is conceivable that Lucia meant: 'When are we to be allowed to *say* who you are?' but more than one person has assured me that there is another explanation proper to the Portuguese environment.

[1] The situation is different from Bernadette's who did *not* understand the words: 'I am the Immaculate Conception' though she had heard the expression. But in 1858 the dogma had been defined only four years previously; whereas devotion to the Immaculate Heart of Mary had been popular long before 1917, and the Immaculate Conception, at any rate, had been the special and almost immemorial devotion of Portugal.

It is, that in Portugal 'Our Lady' is not considered an adequate title for the Blessed Virgin; she must be *defined* as Our Lady of Graces, of Sorrows, of Carmel, of Necessities, of the Rosary. A friend of mine bought a statue of our Lady and the Holy Child and the servants at once asked, '*What* our Lady is she?' The Apparition, then, though well-known to be our Lady, 'defined' herself on October 13 as 'the Lady of the Rosary', though even so saying nothing about the Immaculate Heart. Others, however, whom I questioned, thought this hypothesis to be unnecessary. *Nossa Senhora* is, in fact, and as is clear from the interrogatories, quite a current expression and would amply have sufficed to fix the identity of the vision.

## CHAPTER 2

## 1942: THE LATEST DOCUMENT

LUCIA writes that on July 13, 1917, our Lady further said:

'Make sacrifices for sinners and say often, especially when you make a sacrifice: "Oh Jesus, this is for love of Thee, for the conversion of sinners and in reparation for sins against the Immaculate Heart of Mary."'

She then opened her hands as before, and 'the sheaf of reflected light seemed to penetrate into the earth, and we saw as it were a sea of fire in which were immersed demons, black and bronze, and souls in human form like transparent embers which floated above the flames uplifted by the flames that they themselves emitted and fell back from all sides like sparks in great conflagrations, without weight or equilibrium, among cries and lamentations of pain and despair. This made us horror-struck and trembling with appallment. (It is probably at this moment that I uttered the cry "Ah"! which people said they heard.) The demons could be distinguished by their horrible and disgusting forms of terrifying and unknown animals, transparent like black burning coals.'

Lucia adds that this vision lasted only for a moment, and had it not been for the goodness of our Lady and her promise to take them to heaven they would have died of fright. The vision, then, was given in a moment of time and required to be *translated* to the imagination of the children and, obviously, to that of those to whom it was transmitted. We know, of course, that neither souls nor demons have shapes; and the very expression 'unknown animals' recalls the medieval pictures of devils in hybrid forms. It may indeed be that God presented the idea of 'hell' to the children in the imagery to which pulpit and devotional rhetoric had accustomed them, or, which seems to me more likely, that He directly illuminated their minds as to the terrible and enduring effects of grave unrepented sin, and that Lucia transmitted this illumination to others in the imagery to which she was accustomed and in which she no doubt presented it to herself when reflecting on it. That is normal. We neither can nor wish to deny that a true illumination was granted, though it need not have been visual. Ti Marto witnesses to Lucia's sudden pallor and cry; and hell became almost too much of a preoccupation of Jacinta's. It is invaluable to have 'corroborative' evidence of an assertion, howeve: sincere be the person who makes it.

Lucia then wrote that our Lady proceeded:

'You have seen hell where the souls of sinners go. To save them, the Lord wishes to establish in the world devotion to my Immaculate Heart. If you do what I shall tell you, many souls will be saved and there will be peace. The war [i.e. the 1914-1918 war] is about to end, but if men do not cease to offend God there will begin a worse one in the Pontificate of Pius XI. When you see a night illuminated by an unknown light, know that this is the great sign that God gives you that the punishment of the world is at hand for its so great sins by means of war, famine and persecutions directed against the Church and the Holy Father. To prevent this I shall come to ask for the consecration of Russia to my Immaculate Heart and the Communion of Reparation on the first Saturdays of the month. If my demands are listened to Russia will be converted and there will be peace. Otherwise Russia will spread her errors throughout the world arousing wars and persecutions of the Church. Many good men will be martyred; the Holy Father will have much to suffer; various nations will be annihilated. In the end my Immaculate Heart will triumph. The Holy Father will consecrate Russia to me; Russia will be converted and there will be some peace (*algum paz*).'

It cannot be denied that this narrative has created so many difficulties—again of various sorts—and for so many people, as to cause them to doubt the authenticity of the whole story of 'Fatima'. I want to set forth some of these difficulties as loyally as I can and then to offer my own very tentative considerations, and therefore to give full value to the objections, and the minimum value to my suggestions.

It is said, for example, that the Second World War did not break out under Pius XI but under Pius XII (on September 1, 1939; Pius XII had been elected on March 2); that the second war was not exclusively, or even primarily, due to Russia; that a version of the message for some time current had the 'world' throughout instead of Russia, and 'an impious propaganda' instead of Russia's spreading her errors through the world; that what Lucia originally asked for was the consecration of Russia by the Pope and all the bishops of the world on one and the same day; that our Lady said, *unconditionally*, that if the consecration took place Russia would be converted and there would be no second war; and finally, if Lucia knew all this in 1917, of what use was her knowledge if she was told to keep it secret, and of what use was its proclamation when the second war was already raging?

Lucia has been examined about these and lesser difficulties and insists on what we may call the stronger form of her affirmations. Thus during the war a version of the message was undoubtedly circulated substituting the word 'world' for 'Russia'; this was quasi-officially done, in a chancellery but with ecclesiastical assistance, for 'prudential' reasons, i.e. lest Portugal should seem to be violating her neutrality. Lucia insists that 'Russia' is the only proper word, and it is, in fact, now put back. It seems certain, too, that Lucia wrote to the Holy Father in 1929 saying that 'Our Lady commanded the Holy Father to consecrate Russia to her Immaculate Heart and that he should command all the bishops to do it also in union with him at the same time'. The draft of this letter has been kept, and it certainly contains the words quoted. However, she wrote her draft in a copybook, and it seems hardly probable, as we said above, that she could write elegantly enough for the actual letter to be sent to Rome. If it was written out for her, it is conceivable that the sentence referring to a world-wide simultaneous consecration was omitted as somewhat peremptory and difficult of execution. Though a copy of the letter was shown to the Cardinal Patriarch at Lisbon, Fr. McGlynn says (p. 30) that the Patriarch does not remember that proviso.

Fr. McGlynn explicitly asked Lucia whether the promise that Russia would be converted was absolute or conditional. She said:

'In the end [i.e. of the July text], *absolute*' (p. 92).

'Did the Holy Father consecrate Russia to the Immaculate Heart?'

'He included Russia in the consecration', she said. Then, very humbly, as if wishing she were wrong, she added: 'In the official way that our Lady asked for it? I don't think so.'

Fr. Gardiner, Fr. McGlynn's companion, wishing to make certain of this, reframed the question thus:

'Do you think that our Lady's request has been complied with?'

'As our Lady made it, no. Whether our Lady accepted the consecration made in 1942 as fulfilling her wish I don't know.'

I repeat, there seems to be here a slight hesitation as to the facts. First, Cardinal Cerejeira told Fr. McGlynn that in February 1939 he had received a copy of a letter sent by Lucia to the Bishop of Leiria to this effect—'War is imminent. The sins of men will be washed in their own blood. Those nations will suffer most in the war which tried to destroy the Kingdom of God. Portugal will suffer some of the consequences of war, but, because of the consecration of Portugal to the Immaculate Heart,[1] she would not suffer all of them.' Lucia had declared that the special grace to be awarded for this consecration would be the shortening of the war, and that if the Holy Father wished to see an example of the blessings that this would bring to the world, it could be observed in the case of Portugal.[2] He added that Lucia had herself requested the Pope to carry out our Lady's wish that the world should be consecrated to her Immaculate Heart with special reference to Russia. It was clearly in consequence of this that Pius XII spoke to the Portuguese people on October 31, 1942, consecrating the world to the Immaculate Heart, making a long reference to Russia though not by name. Fr. De Marchi quotes Lucia directly:

'In 1940 I wrote to the bishop referring to the failure to fulfil our Lady's wishes. I wrote: "If only

[1] In 1931, following on the 1930 pastoral of the Bishop of Leiria declaring the story of the Apparitions to be worthy of credence, the Portuguese hierarchy did so join in consecrating the country.

[2] That *some* prophecy about the safety of Portugal was known when the war broke out is certain, because I know a family which, on the strength of it, debated whether they could remain there or go to Canada.

the world knew the moment of grace that is conceded and would do penance!" In the letter which, by order of my spiritual directors, I wrote to the Holy Father in 1940, I exposed the *exact request* of our Lady and asked for the consecration of the world with special mention of Russia.'

It would seem then that there were two stages in Lucia's petitions. She first asked that the Holy Father and all bishops should consecrate Russia on one and the same day. This was not done. Had it been done, Lucia asserts, there would have been no second war, for Russia would have been converted. But, we might ask, would Hitler have been? It is true that Lenin and Trotsky entered Petrograd on April 16, 1917, almost one month before the first apparition and a month after the abdication of the Tsar, and that thenceforward the Bolshevik movement evolved into the Communist régime as we now know it; but the origins of the Second World War were by no means only Russian. Anyhow, the Holy See, despite many a petition made ever since 1900, never had consecrated the world to the Immaculate Heart, though Leo XIII in 1899 had consecrated the world to the Sacred Heart, stirred by the petitions of the holy Mother Mary of the Divine Heart (Gräfin Droste zu Wischering), superior of the Good Shepherd nuns at Oporto. Lucia therefore made her second petition in 1940 asking for the consecration of the *world* 'with special mention of Russia', according to the 'exact request' of our Lady, though I cannot discover when this request was made.

Some theologians have argued that the Pope *could* not consecrate Russia as such because you cannot consecrate a person or a group against their will. But who, in Russia, are men of bad will? Doubtless the Government, and the Communist party as

such. The people are probably as devout to our Lady
as ever they were, and Pius XII said as much; and if
certain 'Orthodox' theologians have of late years
explicitly rejected the dogma of the Immaculate
Conception, I think that that may be because they
want (chiefly for political or other opportunist reasons)
to accentuate all that divides them from the Holy
See. And, after all, the Pope did consecrate the *world*
to the Immaculate Heart, and the world contains
many millions who are not Christians at all. Anyhow,
the Holy See judged it best to act as it did, which is
what Lucia ended by asking, though she manifestly
regretted her original petition not having been complied with. And, I repeat, the promise of the conversion of a nation or even one person, made *unconditionally*, even if they have been consecrated without their
free consent, seems rather mechanical and unlike the
course of Christian history. Calvary itself has not
converted the world which it redeemed.

It is clear, then, that Lucia mentioned Russia to
her bishop in 1929, and, after that, to various ecclesiastics, but nothing was made public till the 1941-1942
document. Asked, on various occasions, what was the
use of making this announcement when the war had
actually begun, especially as the war was to be considered as a *punishment* and it seemed idle to say that
people *would* be punished when they were actually
*being* punished, she said several times that she was
not meant to be a prophetess; that she had not spoken
earlier because 'not finding accurate words in which
to express myself, I would have created such confusion that I might well have spoilt the work of God'
(Fonseca, p. 43); while to Fr. Gardiner (McGlynn,
p. 78) she said that her writings could not be published in their entirety because 'they must contain
private things . . . or things about Russia which the

bishop thinks should not be published' and references to living persons; and to Fr. McGlynn (p. 90), that everything had really been said in 1917, that is, that men must amend their lives and not offend God who was already much offended.[1]

She insists, too, that the Lady mentioned Pius XI by name, and when it was recalled that the war did not begin till Pius XII had been pope for some time, she said that the invasion of Austria and the Anschluss were the real beginning of the war, and that Pius XI had proclaimed this. I do not think that anyone at the time thought of the Anschluss as the actual starting of war, however much more probable it made it: in Rome itself, I remember, it was not spoken of as war.

Lucia seems to have hesitated about the 'great light' that was to illuminate the sky and presage the imminence of war. At first she undoubtedly identified this with the remarkable but not unique Aurora Borealis of January 25-26, 1938, and wrote of it to the bishop that men of science merely tried to regard it as a natural phenomenon: she seems rather to have come back on this, and suggested that God might well have 'used' it as a warning for herself. But now, I believe, she asserts positively that it was *the* light; anyhow, since her information had not then been published, people at large would have been unable to attach any significance to it, though comets are still taken as ominous by simpler minds.

Two interesting suggestions have been made about this question of the war. The first is in the brochure mentioned on page 3 which appeared first in *Streven*. It is, that Lucia, then at Tuy in Spain, took

---

[1] I recall that Lucia said (p. 98) that if people did know the 'secret' it would make no great difference to them. This sounds cynical or despairing: but little children are not cynics, and can't 'despair'.

the Spanish civil war for the prophesied war, and
she will certainly have heard more about the rôle of
Russia in it than we were allowed to. The other is by
Dr. Ernst Karl Winter, in an article entitled 'Die
Russlandbotschaft von Fatima' (*Schweizer Rundschau;*
Heft 4/5, 1948-1949) of which he has kindly sent me a
reprint. He thinks that people are concentrating on
the 'Russian' element in our narrative at the expense
of what Lucia herself declares to have been the central
point of the whole series of Apparitions, namely, the
conversion of sinners and the return of souls to God.
'This idea was repeated in all the Apparitions, that is
why I consider it the principal message.' If I understand Dr. Winter aright, he thinks that the threat of
war may have been given to Lucia in a general form,
and that as time went on she 'crystallised' the notion
into what concerned Russia specifically, especially
after the events in Portugal and the communistic
and anarchic revolutions which preceded the advent
of Dr. Salazar in 1926-1927.

One cannot commit oneself to any such explanation as certain; but, for my part, I would not feel in
any way disconcerted to find that God, through our
Lady, communicated a truth to what mystical theologians have called the 'centre of the soul', provi-
dentially guiding Lucia's mind and imagination to
'shape' it in such ideas and forms, and to state it in
such words, as progressively came to be at her dis-
posal.[1] Thus she would have been seeing more deeply

---

[1] That remarkable man H. Jaegen, in his *Mystic Life of Graces* (translated by Rev. W. J. Anderson; Burns Oates, 1936)—he had been an
engineer, a soldier, a banker and Landtag deputy for ten years and
died on January 26, 1919, aged seventy-seven, and apparently a true
mystic—recalls that God is not bound to act on the imagination through
the senses, but can do so directly, or again, on the intelligence. If He
does this, the imagination, which is the normal instrument of the
understanding, 'at once gives to these ideas a corresponding visible

and indeed more accurately into what had originally been given her and yet, not being exempt from the psychological laws that govern the human mind, she could have made all those innocent mistakes which, we saw (pp. 8-11), quite honest recipients of genuine 'revelations' can make. Lucia again and again asserted that there was much she 'couldn't explain'; she was proud of her memory, but it was sometimes at fault—she might be unable, for example, to remember when she asked our Lady for a miracle, she says she could not *draw* figures that appeared by the sun—'the changes that took place were all changes of light; I can't explain'; she could not give our Lady's exact words—'it was rather the sense that came to me and I put what I understood into words. It is not easy to explain this.' It is clear that she expanded the instantaneous vision of hell into quite an elaborate symbolical description; I should not consider that any of her message was injured if Lucia ended by feeling she had known and seen from the very beginning all that she at a later moment knew—for instance, if she put back the vision of the Immaculate Heart proper to much earlier—to the June Apparition of 1917. All agree that she is an unimaginative, uninventive, sincere and 'ordinary' person, and supremely indifferent as to whether people believe her or not; but she seems to me to reconstruct her memories not a little unconsciously, sincerely, yet not unnaturally.

I am, then, inclined to give much value to the

form'. The imagination therefore *adds* something to the divine communication, but there is no harm in that, since God foresaw that *that* seer would act imaginatively in *that* way and did not prevent him from doing so (p. 145). St. Teresa, speaking of 'seen' visions, says: 'Although I call it a "picture", you must not suppose that it looks like a painting. Christ appears as a living person.' Yet even so, she declares that she has never seen a 'corporeal' vision of our Lord.

conversations that Lucia relates as having followed the various Apparitions, allowing always for verbal modifications and occasional uncertainties as to date. After the vision of hell, Jacinta remained overcome.

'What are you thinking of?' Lucia asked.

'Of hell and the poor sinners. How sorry I am for the souls that go to hell. And people burning there like coals. . . . Oh Lucia, why doesn't our Lady show hell to sinners? Why didn't you ask her to show hell to these people? They certainly wouldn't go on sinning any more.'

'I didn't think of it', Lucia said.

Jacinta cried: 'Oh, Lucia, oh Francisco! we must go on praying, praying, to save souls from hell. So many go there! . . . what sort of sins send people to hell?'

'I don't know. Perhaps not going to Mass, stealing, swearing. . . .'

'And just for that do they go to hell?'

'Yes, it's a sin.'

'Oh why don't they go to Mass—it's not difficult.'

We can trust that Lucia, who tried to explain how our Lord was present in every consecrated particle, was able to explain the difference between repented and unrepented sin, and that no assessment can be made as to the relative numbers of lost and saved. It is certain that Jacinta was increasingly preoccupied with 'making sacrifices' for sinners; Lucia tells how on one scorchingly hot day they were tormented by thirst; so long as they could, they offered this as sacrifice; but at last Lucia fetched some water; the two younger ones refused it, so Lucia poured it away. Again, one noon the crickets and frogs increased their exasperating chatter. Jacinta said:

'Lucia, tell those things to keep quiet! My head aches so.'

Francisco said: 'Don't you want to suffer for sinners?'

'Yes, yes! Don't tell them to stop, Lucia!'

It may well be that, as we suggested, when Fr. Faustino Ferreira appeared and 'taught' them how to make sacrifices, he regulated imprudent practices such as these; Lucia put her whole trust in him, and regarded him as a true 'director'.

Jacinta developed, too, a real 'devotion' for the Holy Father. He and his anxieties became a recurrent theme in her talk. One day, by the well, she asked Lucia (who with Francisco had been looking for some wild honey) if she had not seen the Holy Father.

'No.'

'I don't know how it was, but I saw the Holy Father in a very big house, kneeling before a table with his hands before his face, crying. He went to the door of the house and there were lots of people there throwing stones and cursing and saying horrible words. Poor Holy Father! we must pray for him too.'

Again, at the Cabeço Jacinta asked if Lucia did not see 'all those roads and fields full of people crying with hunger and with nothing to eat? And the Holy Father in a church praying to the Immaculate Heart of Mary?'

My impression is that Jacinta was a much more sensitive and imaginative little girl than Lucia, perhaps more rapid in her sympathy with the sufferings of others and more vivid in her picturing them. However isolated was the life of these peasants, they cannot have been wholly unaware of the horrors of war and the distresses of the Holy Father. The parish-priest, surely, will have spoken of them in his sermons; the elders went to towns where markets and fairs were held and where they will have heard many a rumour and afterwards have talked, during the long evenings, about what they heard; and people who cannot read are often better at imagining (and certainly at remembering) than those whose brains are cluttered up with what they get from newspapers, and whose imaginations are inflamed by cinemas. Perhaps this intensely vivid realising of suffering, both temporal and everlasting, was needed if Jacinta was to have the courage to endure the really dreadful sacrifices which were her vocation. Francisco, too, was called to suffer terribly, and he, too, was very sensitive for all his vivacity; all personal impressions are, evidently, no more than that, yet I cannot help acknowledging that I seem to recognise in him a more directly mystical life than that, even, of his sister.

## CHAPTER 3

# THE DEVELOPMENT OF THE CULTUS

WE may now very briefly recall the development of the shrine. On May 3, 1922, the Bishop of Leiria issued the pastoral in which he said that he could not remain indifferent to the pilgrims who came in ever-increasing numbers to the Cova da Iria. The children were no more there; the place had no natural beauty and every inconvenience; the civil authorities had tried every means, including violence, to prevent people going there; the clergy had studiously avoided all encouragement. He set up a commission, therefore, to investigate the facts.

In October, 1926, the diocese of Leiria was commemorating the seventh centenary of St. Francis of Assisi, and on that occasion the Apostolic Nuncio visited the Cova and made a report to Rome, and on January 21, 1927, a votive Mass was granted to Fatima. In July of that year, the bishops presided for the first time, after the erection of the Stations of the Cross along the road, at an official ceremony at the Cova. Meanwhile the Commission reached its conclusion that the Apparitions were worthy of credence (see p. 5) and that a 'cultus' should be permitted.

On May 13, 1937, the Apostolic Nuncio presided at the first Portuguese national pilgrimage at which it is calculated that half a million persons were present. Exactly a year later a second such pilgrimage took place in fulfilment of the Hierarchy's promise to organise this, if our Lady would save Portugal from the horrors of the civil war being waged on her very frontiers. On October 13, 1939, the Cardinal Patriarch presided at a pilgrimage which was made to implore peace for Portugal; and from April 8 to 13, 1942, the Girls' Catholic Youth movement arranged the procession of our Lady's statue to Lisbon and back. On May 13 another national pilgrimage celebrated the 'silver jubilee' of the Apparitions and on October 31 of that year the Holy Father consecrated the world to the Immaculate Heart of Mary and broadcast his address to Portugal, speaking in Portuguese. Independently even of this warmly outspoken address, it is well known how deep is the devotion of Pius XII to Our Lady of Fatima. Later still, he sent Cardinal Aloisi Masella as his Legate to crown the statue of Our Lady of Fatima, which he did in the presence of some 800,000 persons.

On this occasion it was decided that the crowned statue of our Lady should be carried to Lisbon and across the Tagus, and then home by a different route. The idea was very apt, since in 1946 Portugal was celebrating the third centenary of John IV's proclamation of our Lady as Queen of Portugal, since when, I think, the Portuguese kings never themselves wore the crown.[1]

A grand motor-car with glass sides was prepared but the population would have none of that. The statue should be carried by human arms from place to place, spending the night in one parish church after another. It reached Bombarral, a village once noted for its indifference or anti-clericalism. Now a lady of that place had asked a friend to buy six doves (they were, rather, pigeons) in the ordinary Lisbon market and to send them in a basket to Bombarral.

[1] In what follows I quote from pages 146, 147 of *Portuguese Pilgrimage* (Sheed and Ward, 1949).

When it was opened, one had died (or was not to be found); two, speckled ones, flew away; the remaining three fluttered to the pedestal of the statue and perched there. People had placed flowers all round it and feared the birds would disarrange them; they tried to shoo them away. They fluttered up a little, but always returned. The procession moved forward. . . . You may not know what such a procession is like! The crowds exult, applaud, wave handkerchiefs. Bells clash; bombs burst; rockets hiss and crackle. The doves must surely be tied there? But no—they would flutter up from time to time, circle over the people—one actually perched on a man who could not believe they were real—and always they returned to our Lady. From December 5 to 7, the statue remained in the Lisbon Fatima church, the doves at its feet or sometimes on the canopy of the Patriarch's throne. The statue was then taken to the cathedral, outside which a friend of mine was standing in the rain from 9 p.m. to 1 a.m. when the procession arrived. He watched one of the doves fly up to one of the great towers, and then, apparently considering its duty done, it flew away. (At this point there are slightly different accounts of the behaviour of the doves, due, perhaps, to the position of the various onlookers; and the same is true for what happened when the statue got across the Tagus.)

On this same day, by a coincidence that you can view as you please, in the church of the Immaculate Conception at Rio de Janeiro a dove flew into the church during the sermon and perched on the High Altar cross. There it remained throughout the ceremony and afterwards photographers and press men were sent for, and in spite of them and the crowds that thronged up to inspect it, the bird remained there imperturbable. This was fully reported, with a photograph, in the Lisbon *Novidades* for January 9, 1947.

When the *festa* of December 8 was over, the statue went off across the Tagus, which is very wide there. Apparently only one dove accompanied the illuminated barge. It had, in any case, to endure the honking of the horns and the shriek of the sirens from a thousand fishing-smacks, motor-boats, and steamers which surrounded it. At the seminary of Almeida, next day, this dove stood all the morning on the pedestal, heedless of the throngs, to say nothing of the children whom the seminarians lifted up to kiss the foot of the statue. Here one of my informants filmed it. As the procession left, it flew on to the roof of the seminary and the procession left without it. One of the students, however, picked it up and let it fly; after a while it saw the statue already distant, flew after it and perched on the pedestal again. Two other doves were afterwards let loose; the original one disappeared; the two remained; others arrived.

At Torres Novas, on the way home, a small child (related to one of my informants) asked his parents to give our Lady some birds from his own dovecote. Six were sent out. Three dark-coloured ones flew back. Three white ones accompanied the statue to Fatima where the bishop caused a small dovecote to be built for them.

This incident is so richly documented, photographed and filmed and involves so many eye-witnesses that it cannot but be accepted substantially, and I find it enchanting, and just the sort of manifestation of heavenly humour that seems to me suited to the genial Portuguese people.

A separate chapter, for which I cannot yet collect adequate material, could be written about the

'Travelling Madonna'; for the Fatima statue has been on many a voyage, and it, or its replica, may quite possibly go round the world. Westminster itself has one, which will, I understand, visit the diocesan parish churches, and no better welcome can be given her than an effort to see deep into her message and to act on it.

# EPILOGUE

THE previous pages are only too likely to contain inaccuracies, partly due directly to faulty judgements of my own, and partly because the books I have read so often fail to say the same thing, or because an author may generalise or decorate his evidence. The following pages are even more likely to contain errors, because in them I hope to extract what seems to me the essential 'Message' of Fatima, and here, personal preferences or surmises run a still greater risk of error.

To some extent, each narrative (that of 1917 and that of 1942) stands by itself—we do not so clearly see in the former that the message was meant for the world; and what Lucia insists on is repentance and the rosary. Moreover, in each there is an element of the pictorial, and of the specific, which may distract us from the essence of the message. Thus those who know only a little about 'Fatima' are sure to allude to the 'miracle of the sun'; and, there was the specific, concrete request of our Lady that a 'chapel' should be built. It has indeed been built, and vast reconstructions of the locality, for which the Government is responsible, are being made. Sentimentally, we cannot but regret the total alteration of the Cova da Iria from what it originally was, though we see that regulation of the enormous traffic is necessary and it is good that commercialism will be excluded from the vicinity. Still, had the Government intervened, I would have preferred it to construct an aqueduct or a pumping-system! The basilica itself was built entirely out of the unsolicited alms of the Faithful—I understand that the Bishop of Leiria has always refused to launch a general 'appeal'; and it would have been pleasant to think that it was the Faithful, too, who were responsible for any modifications of the Cova itself which seemed really desirable.

As for the complexus of 'atmospheric phenomena' of which the 'miracle of the sun' was the most impressive—however preternatural its origin, it remains but a 'sign', pointing to something beyond itself and inviting us to transcend it so soon as possible. Lucia herself insisted, as we saw, that in every apparition our Lady constantly called for amendment of life, and asked for the recitation of the rosary which, Lucia said, was a very good way to help those who did not know how to pray to draw nearer to God.

The second mass of evidence contains two totally new themes—the main one being devotion to the Immaculate Heart of Mary; and the subordinate one, the conversion of Russia. (The vision of hell can be linked, in retrospect, with the warning against unrepented sin.) We recalled that our Lady herself can reveal no new truth of faith or morals, and in any case, devotion to her Immaculate Heart is no new thing. St. John Eudes had obtained permission for his Mass in honour of her Heart even before that of the Sacred Heart of our Lord, and St. Margaret Mary found it being celebrated in her convent at Paray when she entered it. Even before entering it, she had seen her own heart—a tiny heart—between those of Jesus and Mary; and St. Francis de Sales, devising a 'crest' for the Visitation Order, spoke of those Hearts as *cet unique Coeur*. The most, therefore, that Lucia could ask for would be a wider extension and a better understanding of that devotion; and we do not think there should be any real danger of the devotion to our Lord's Sacred Heart and the Immaculate Heart of His Mother being taken as *parallel*

—let alone, the same in kind. True, authors have thought it necessary to alter the expression given by Lucia to the message of the Angel, lest she should sound as saying that our Lady's merits are infinite, as His are (cf. p. 149). But all are aware that adoration is due to the Person of our Lord, true man and true God, because of the hypostatic union, and that no such adoration is given to our Lady, devotion to whose heart is purely mystical. And this is well symbolised when, after the great processions of her statue at Fatima, it is placed modestly to one side, and the attention of all is rivetted to the Offering of the Holy Sacrifice and the reception of Holy Communion.[1]

But we have found that—perhaps inevitably—human curiosity has fastened on the 'secret' and even to wonder what is in the yet unopened document. Now the first two parts of the secret contain, as we saw, nothing new. 'Hell' is no new doctrine; nor that our Lady is Immaculate. It is not novel or startling *information* that our Lady proposed to impart to us, but rather, a challenge to look more deeply into what we already know. It need not surprise us that the children were told to say nothing about what had been granted to them; Lucia quite frankly said that she would not have had words in which to express herself properly, and, to the end, that she could give only the 'sense' of our Lady's message.[2] This encourages one to think that the 'secrecy' of that message may have concerned the *intensity* with which the

[1] We are not forgetting the doctrine of the Mystical Body of Christ, in which our Lady holds a unique place: but we recall, too, how two Prayers in the Mass in honour of her sorrows (Friday in Passion Week) insist upon those saints who keep her faithful company at the foot of the Cross.

[2] Nor could anyone have understood the *Russia* motif in the middle of the 'Kaiser's War'.

children were made to understand certain truths, rather than anything which could be crystallised into clear ideas or put into forms of words. Speaking purely for myself, I would not be disconcerted if our Lady had made them realise the intensity of her purity and love, which, later on, Lucia 'described' as her Immaculate Heart, somewhat as she expanded the instantaneous perception of hell pictorially, and making use of an imagery which is certainly not of equal service to all (see R. P. Rambaud, p. 90. Fr. Sertillanges, O.P., also has written that the medieval *imagery* connected with the dogma of hell may not assist modern minds to appreciate that dogma.) After all, we no more use our Lord's own way of describing heaven as a feast shared with the Hebrew Patriarchs. Hence it might well be that the third part of the 'secret' does not contain anything that would flatter our curiosity and our somewhat materialist desire for the definite and the concrete.

Still, it may be said that 'Russia' and its conversion and a particular method of consecrating it to our Lady's Heart, with the unconditional consequence of 'no second war', are definite and concrete enough. The fact remains, however, that the Holy See did *not* act on Lucia's first request, and we can hardly be surprised. I repeat, that request was one among very many; it was very 'exorbitant' to mobilise the world's hierarchies and to persuade them to perform a certain act of religion on one particular day would be incredibly difficult and not according, I think, to the traditional methods of the Holy See; and, as I said, the conversion of a whole nation, or even of its Government, unconditionally promised as a consequence of such a consecration, has a taste of magic about it. It seems to me that what the Holy See actually did—to consecrate the world to the

Immaculate Heart of Mary, with 'special mention' of Russia—is more easily imaginable and perhaps theologically more acceptable, especially as no special consequence is *mechanically* expected from it, let alone promised.

'Russia', after all, is a terribly important fact, but a temporal one; she will not last for ever, any more than other tyrannies have lasted. But at the moment she does stand as symbol for what is anti-God, anti-Christ, indeed, anti-human, more than any other force of which we are conscious. But what Russia symbolises is not incarnate in herself alone; in practically all countries there are groups of determined men who propose to win absolute power for the State (in reality, for themselves) to the exclusion of God, the spirit, and the conscience personal to each man. But even a small group of clear-headed and determined men can influence immense masses of men who are confused in mind and without determination. For nothing but a vacillating will, or apathy, attends upon minds that are vague. Therefore the two great wars that we have witnessed are themselves little more than symbols, or at least symptoms, of what the world may expect if there is no clearer vision than there is now, nor a radical change of heart and will.

If, then, we are to see the two wars as parables in action, so to say, we have to realise that what lies behind them is not merely an affair of economics or of frontiers, but of *sin*. We can hardly be astonished if God takes (we dare to say) drastic steps to re-awaken in us the sense of sin. Who should fail to see what is sinful and indeed Satanic in a world where nightmares have become commonplaces? We read with sorrow of the tortures inflicted on the bodies of prisoners or other victims in bygone times; but what was the dislocation of limbs upon a rack compared with the scientific breaking-down of minds which has now been practised not in one country only? We have called ourselves 'civilised', and have invented the gas-chamber and the concentration-camp. And even if these exhibitions of calculated cruelty should cease, the possibility of a world in which the State is absolute is a very real one, with the corollaries of farcical trials and confessions. But when all is said and done, these things are but the shadow of the enduring consequences of unrepented sin, which are displayed to us by the doctrine of Hell.

Our Lady, therefore, was commissioned to recall to us the extreme of sin, and, in the example of her sinless heart, the extreme of holiness. So the message of Fatima is very far from ending in a threat. And it is impossible to doubt that that message began at once to make its way through the country in which it first was spoken. Let us grant that the Portuguese temperament and tradition are different from ours; we may, therefore, not see in Portuguese 'religion' all those elements that we expect among ourselves, just as any southerner might be all too justified in many a northern land if he thought religion was largely 'respectable' and hand in glove with the comfortable and 'moderate'. It would in any case be impossible to disentangle the part of Portugal's transformation which is directly due to Fatima from that which is directly due to human causes. That transformation is not nearly complete; but we feel hopeful that it will continue owing to influences undoubtedly proceeding from, or liberated by, the events at Fatima. The Government, though responsible for order where there was chaos, creation where there were ruins, is not, as such, 'Catholic'. But it provides, so to say, the wire which the Faith can electrify, and this is happening. Who, but a few years ago, could have expected in Portugal retreats for doctors, engineers, lawyers? Who, the great retreats for young working-men, at Fatima? Who could have foreseen those contingents of young men and girls who go into the thinly-populated areas of the land to prepare the way for the priest—alas, such is still the shortage of priests that whole regions are practically unvisited by them and deprived, therefore, of the Sacraments! My earnest hope is, that should Portugal be destined to further political and social changes, forces such as I have briefly alluded to will *not* change, save but to be increased, and form a strong barrier against those other Satanic forces that still exist there and are only too anxious to reintroduce the disastrous chaos of those sixteen years. But since the message of Fatima is not for Portugal only, so neither shall I try even to outline the spiritual changes visible, and to be hoped for, in that land. We know very well that a 'change of heart' is quite beyond any power of our own; that our hearts *ought* to be different we also know, and we see it all the more clearly when we reflect upon her whose sinless heart was so akin to her Son's most Sacred Heart. And if it be said that the 'amendment of our lives', and 'advance towards holiness' are truths so simple as to have become practically banal, it may well be *because* these vitally and everlastingly all-important matters have come to sound banalities in our ears, that God chose a method so extraordinary as the series of Apparitions at Fatima and the lessons afterwards deduced from them, in order to startle us out of our somnolence. 'Give light to my eyes, lest ever I sleep in death.'

I have, then, constantly invoking our Lady by her latest world-known title, 'of Fatima', tried to write that story as honestly as I could, saying, it is true, very little about Lucia, whose exterior vocation seems

to be accomplished, though she is still alive, but
having contemplated with grateful happiness the
action of grace upon the sensitive child Jacinta, and
on her brother who does, indeed, seem to me trans-
formed from light to light ; and having tried to
reach, across their words, the spiritual and living
gift that was vouchsafed to them. And I can but once
more ask pardon for any mistake as to fact, or inter-
pretation of fact, into which I may have fallen.